So WHAT do you RECKON?

ROBERT G. BARRETT

So WHAT do you RECKON?

HarperCollins*Publishers*

HarperCollins*Publishers*

First published in Australia in 1997
Reprinted in 1998, 1999
by HarperCollins*Publishers* Pty Limited
ACN 009 913 517
A member of the HarperCollins*Publishers* (Australia) Pty Limited Group
http://www.harpercollins.com.au

HarperCollins*Publishers*
25 Ryde Road, Pymble, Sydney, NSW 2073, Australia
31 View Road, Glenfield, Auckland 10, New Zealand
77-85 Fulham Palace Road, London W6 8JB, United Kingdom
Hazelton Lanes, 55 Avenue Road, Suite 2900, Toronto, Ontario M5R 3L2
and 1995 Markham Road, Scarborough, Ontario M1B 5M8, Canada
10 East 53rd Street, New York NY 10022, USA

National Library of Australia Cataloguing-in-Publication data:

Barrett, Robert G.
So what do you reckon?
ISBN 0 7322 5961 4.
1. Australian wit and humour – 20th century.
2. Australia – Social life and customs – 20th century.
3. Australia – Social conditions – 20th century. I. Title.
A823.3

Printed in Australia by Griffin Press Pty Ltd on 80gsm Econoprint

9 8 7 6 5 4 3 99 00 01 02

CONTENTS

A word from the Possum Lady regarding Team Norton. The following T-shirts are now available:

You Wouldn't Be Dead For Quids
The Boys From Binjiwunyawunya
Mele Kalikimaka Mr Walker
The Day Of The Gecko
Davo's Little Something
White Shoes White Lines and Blackie
Rider On The Storm
Guns And Rose

Plus, Team Norton caps in black and green with gold embroidery.

T-shirts: $32.00. Caps: $28.00. (Includes postage.)

Send cheque or money order to:
Psycho Possum Productions
P.O. Box 3348
Tamarama NSW 2026.

The Possum Lady also said thank you. She's got most of her teeth fixed. Now she hopes to get a surgical boot and a glass eye.

The author is donating a percentage of the royalties from this book to Greg Mulder and Debbie Green from the Wombat Research and Rescue Project, Tumbi Umbi, NSW Central Coast.

Visit Bob's official web site
and the home of Team Norton at:
http://www.RobertGBarrett.com

INTRODUCTION

Anybody trying to crack it, especially as a writer, needs or gets a break some time. I'm often asked what was my break? Bobbing up on the *Midday Show*, *60 Minutes*, *Australian Story*? Taking those two strippers to the Sydney Writers Festival? These things help, but they don't pay the bank manager. No. My break was writing a column for *People* magazine. In fact, it was more than a break. It saved me. And if you happen to read this JJ, thanks mate. I owe you one.

At one stage of my brilliant career, I had three books published and was in between royalties cheques working as a kitchen hand at a restaurant in Terrigal; exactly like the one in *Between the Devlin and the Deep Blue Seas*. I had a slight altercation with the ex-kitchen hand, a well-known alleged coke dealer. Subsequently, I was charged with assault occasioning actual bodily harm. It was a stew, but I was half expecting something like this because I'd had a fallout with some coppers in a surf club up my way who threatened to get me over a letter I wrote to the editor of a local newspaper. This was their chance. I beat the assault charge fair and square, then the police arrested me again when the verdict was handed down for offensive behaviour. It was alleged that I swore at the plaintiff. The magistrate said, 'I didn't see anything. I didn't hear anything. Case dismissed.' My barrister said, 'I didn't hear anything and I was sitting next to him. What did he say?' And this Gosford copper said, 'I read his lips.' If you don't believe me, read the court transcripts. They're good blokes, the cops on the central coast. Then they flung me in a paddy wagon to be driven 500 metres from Gosford courthouse to Gosford gaol so they could fingerprint me and put me through the whole rigmarole again. Naturally, I beat this charge too and I had a good case against them for malicious arrest and perjury. But the legal fees wiped me out — including the royalties cheque I was waiting for — and, unfortunately, I had to throw the towel in. Plus, I lost my job in the kitchen as well.

So there I am, in my late forties, out of gaol and out of work. Three books published and stone motherless broke. I was honestly wondering if it was all worthwhile when, from out of the blue, I got a phone call from Peter Olszewski, the editor at *People*. Was I interested in writing a column for the magazine? Was I what. I was desperate. But I said I'd never written a column before. JJ said, 'Don't worry, write four columns and if they're any good we'll run it for six months. What do you want to call the column?' I said, 'I don't know. What do you reckon?' JJ said, 'That'll do' and strined it to 'So What Do Ya Reckon?' Whatever he called it, it went for just over two years and the steady money got me out of the kitchens and out of the shit.

I have to admit I can't ever remember buying a copy of *People*. To me it was some kind of blue collar *Penthouse* with heaps of tits and bums, a giant crossword puzzle and something splashed across the cover like: GIANT SEA TURTLE RAPES SCUBA DIVER. I also wasn't sure of my political persuasion. Somewhere to the left of Fidel Castro, the right of Joh Bjelke-

Petersen and above Eddie Vortex. I also knew that, being a WHAMWASH — a white, heterosexual, Australian male with a sense of humour — no matter what I wrote I'd get bombarded with social definitions by the ersatz meritocracy, the stupefyingly boring politically correct. Racist, sexist, crypto-fascist, neo-Nazi etc. You know, the usual self-righteous, pedestrian cant. Yet there was certainly no shortage of things to write about. The environment, drugs, crime, black problems, police shootings. John Laws, Ron Casey, Derryn Hinch, Mike Carlton. People being crushed to death under the weight of their own ego and the nation in a malaise. You wouldn't be a digger if you didn't try to help. Even if it was only through a column in a tits-and-bums magazine like *People*. So away I went. A sort of a Joe Carioca with a typewriter, seeing just how many politically correct dates I could put a rocket up, with the help of an old saying written across my rocket launcher. Many a true word said in jest.

JJ left *People* and the column eventually fizzled out. By then, however, I was just about over the hump and now, if I can write a book a year, I can survive reasonably well. And you never know, if John Singleton and Snail Productions ever get Les Norton up and running on TV I might even finish with a few extra dollars in my kick.

I brought out a book called *Rider On The Storm*. It was mainly short stories and articles that I'd written early in the piece, plus some columns I wrote for *Nine To Five* magazine when I was living in Bondi researching *The Day Of The Gecko*. It went well and a lot of people have asked me why don't I bring out a book of my old *People* columns? To be honest, I'd almost forgotten about them; it was years since I wrote the things. They'd have to be a bit old hat by now. I thought about it, then crawled under the house, dragged out all the cartons of old magazines and went through them again. I'm buggered if I know. They might be a bit old hat, but they are still relevant to what is going on today. A few things have changed. But the environment's stuffed worse than ever, there's more heroin than ever and it's cheaper, crime's now a growth industry, the police are shooting people right on Bondi Beach and the blacks are still screaming blue murder about everything and anything. Lawsie's still blathering away on air wanting to hang greenies, Ron Casey finally hit critical mass, Derryn's wandering the desert and Mike Carlton's back with the rest of the silk worms on the ABC. It's almost as if I'd written them yesterday. So I thought, okay, I'll bring a book of them out — if only for my women readers. You know, despite having one of my books described as the 'scatological nadir of the pile' by some bag on the *Canberra Times*, and, 'Insidiously revolting… Pray God this never reaches the international market' by some other scrubber on the *Sydney Morning Herald*, I'm proud to say that I have got a heap of women readers. Almost half. They've probably never read *People,* same as I've never read *New Idea*. They already know what a sensuous, romantic novelist I am. Now's their chance to know that I was a fairly dab hand as a columnist too. Regardless of that giant gee-up in *Nine To Five*. So, as far as I'm concerned, this one's for the ladies. Bless them.

I have to add that a lot of the columns came with cartoons and photos that I took and without them they do lose a certain ambience; columns such as 'Sleaze stays when the party's over', 'Me nude! You must be stark raving mad' and 'What are you laughin' at?' And, like I said earlier, I wrote them a long time ago. Since then I don't punt any more, I drink very little beer and I've almost lost interest in rugby league. One thing the columns never lost, however, is how I tried to show what a lot of humbug and deceit this so-called political correctness is. And

I'm pleased to see people are finally starting to wake up and beginning to ignore it. Political correctness is nothing more than dialectic sanitisation and truth distortion, foisted on us by a minority of tedious academics and pseudo intellectuals for their own self-gratification. In other words: The Witness Syndrome. Look at me everybody. Aren't I wonderful? You wouldn't hear me saying or even thinking something like that. They live in their own nugatory little worlds stuffed full of their own self-importance, their backsides burning with warm inner glow, their heads shoved firmly in the moral high ground. They've never done a day's work in their lives and wouldn't know the real world if it jumped out of a box and shoved a red-hot pinch bar up their blurters. But, worst of all, they can't laugh at the world or themselves and they hate anybody that can. I could write more about these humourless nonentities, trying to clone us into their own miserable image. But why bother? So I left it to a writer more succinct and wiser than me. George Saintsbury. He reckons, 'Nothing is more curious than the almost savage hostility that humour excites in those who lack it.'

So what do you reckon?

Robert G. Barrett
August 1997

So WHY doesn't JACK THE LAD get a REAL JOB?

Writing in Australia isn't quite the glitzy, glamorous life it's all cracked up to be.

Apart from some yuppies in advertising and say, Colleen McCullough and Thomas Keneally who have cracked it overseas, writing for a living in Oz at times can be like an elephant's foreskin. Quite a drawback.

You're forever broke, trying to exist on royalties cheques which arrive twice a year.

And drunken council workers and concreters with brains as big as the piece of chocolate inside a Jaffa think you're Jack The Lad, having a top time getting paid millions for doing nothing.

They get the Edgar Britts and want to fight you.

Being a bachelor living on the NSW Central Coast away from any semblance of social life doesn't help all that much either.

I shouldn't whinge. Being broke here doesn't necessarily mean you're lonely. There's always someone popping in to see you and have a bit of a chat — field officers from the CES wanting to know why you can't get a job; dragoons from the sheriff's office wanting to take away your car and furniture; lemons from the bank in ill-fitting suits wanting to repossess your home.

And now and again some of the biggest coppers you've ever seen, with batons out, asking if you would mind coming down to the station to answer a few questions.

You get women, too. Hordes of horrible, screeching divorcees that look like they take ugly medicine then get beaten with an ugly stick, along with their equally horrible, uncontrollable anklebiters.

This doesn't mean there's any love there or they think you look like Jason Donovan. These beasts would move in with the Phantom of the Opera if they thought they could get a roof over their heads and somewhere to dump their pointy-headed, snotty-nosed little monsters.

Amidst all this rattle you try to write a book. You realise your bi-annual royalties cheques wouldn't feed an Ethiopian apprentice jockey, you can't get the 'jam roll' any more and, worse, you're just a common or garden writer. That means I write stuff the average punter can understand and enjoy, not to impress the wine-and-cheese set or the Arts Council. That also means I can't get literary grants — the writers' dole.

So you have to get a job. Work doesn't worry me. I did heaps of it before I got hold of a typewriter. But jobs on the Central Coast are harder to find than kosher butcheries in Libya.

I did find one — catering hygiene supervisory officer in an international resort, as the Yanks could put it. In other words, scrubbing pots and pans in the kitchen of a would-be up-market motel.

Now I said I don't mind work, but if nothing else I do have my pride. There was no way I was going to let this hillbilly owner know he had an author working in his kitchen.

So I put my name down in the book as Manuel Barretti and I said I was Portuguese. I was happy enough cleaning dishes, pushing a mop and 'si-ing' and 'que-ing' and 'me no understand-ing' my way around the place when the boss twigged I was an Aussie. Having a typical Central Coast sense of humour, he thought I was having a go at him so the racist bastard gave me the lemon.

From there it was on to an even bigger, grungier pit at The Entrance with a kitchen that looked like Dr Jekyll's lab and with workmates who were a bunch of wimps all terrified of losing their jobs.

Having no chops, I stuck it out, scrubbing burnt pots big enough to house two families of Pakistanis, and emptying Otto bins in the rain with maggots.

I don't like to use the word 'maggots'. It turns you off your food. Let's say baby flies. Hordes of baby flies crawling up my arms and into my gloves and shoes.

The managers knew they had the wimps terrified and treated them accordingly. They tried it with me one night. I had a blue with a little ponce over the radio, so I let him have a banana soufflé for a hat and told them what they could do with their bloody job, maggots … er, I mean, baby flies and all.

On to another restaurant in Terrigal, where … well let's just say, the things that happened to me and the things I saw going on are well worth writing a book about. And believe me, I shall.

Yet there's always that light at the end of the tunnel — even if it is only another train coming at you. I got my head in this American women's magazine called *Alaska Men*, a sort of saucy, up-market, lonely hearts glossy.

Believe me, I wasn't looking for a bride. On my money I need a wife and family like Quasimodo needs a body shirt. I honestly thought it was an invite to a free drink when a planeload of them got out here. And I'm telling you, I'd swim across a lake full of piranhas with a cut leg if there was free piss on the other side.

Instead of a free drink, I got boxes of letters from women all over the USA. Some of them weren't bad sorts either. I suggested to my publishers we send some of them a copy of my first book and see what they think. It might even be a way of back-dooring my books into America.

As a bit of a gimmick I said that if they liked the book they should send me a T-shirt, because the Seppos do have the best T-shirts. Before I knew it, I had a box full of grouse Yank T-shirts and proposals of marriage. They also liked my first book, bad language, swearing, Australian slang and all.

The good people at *People* got to hear about it, too. They were so impressed with my non-sexist attitude they asked me to write a column. Would I like to write a column for the magazine that has the biggest, bounciest, most beautiful women in the land? Would I bloody what? To say I was chuffed would be the understatement of the year.

So what will I call it, and what will a concupiscent curmudgeon like me write about? I can't just plug my books every week and lie about what a good bloke I am.

I could be a sort of thinking man's Paul Hogan. Maybe more, a blue-collar Leo Schofield. How about Derryn Hinch without the irritable bowel syndrome? I don't really know.

I know I do hate hypocrites and self-opinionated, grandiose tall poppies. I'm not just into saving the planet and wildlife. I'm an environmental Nazi and blow up if someone so much as steps on an ant.

I'm a corny, flag-waving patriot and love my country and reckon we're all entitled to a quid, so it irks me when I see banks spending millions of dollars on paintings and furnishings while they're putting farmers off their land.

I just lerrrve feminists and people like the Women Against Rape In War holed up in their collectives around Balmain and Glebe. I'd love to be stranded on a desert island with Germaine Greer and Shere Hite: provided I had a baseball bat, some rope and 5000 litres of boiling chicken fat.

I don't know what I'll write about. Maybe the good readers of *People* will write to me saying they like my column and suggest something.

Others might write to say my column smells like grandpa's socks and suggest I stick my typewriter where the sun don't shine. I'm not above criticism.

But I do know I'm looking forward to it. Rest assured I'll be giving it my best shot every week.

One thing's for certain: No matter what I write about, it can't possibly be any worse than my books.

I MIGHT be a RACIST, but...

I see Trish Goddard is about to have a baby: I think this is a good thing.

I'm all for motherhood and the family unit, and the more bonny Aussie babies I see bouncing around the more I like it.

Of course, the fact that Ms Goddard isn't married makes no difference; where once when your boyfriend got you up the stick, these children born out of wedlock were referred to as 'illegitimate' or 'bastards'. In these more enlightened times these little ones are called 'love children'.

No matter what it is, boy or girl, I hope both mother and child are fit and healthy and do well.

Anyway, I'm sitting on the brasco the other day, pondering and looking for something to read when I pick up an old copy of the *Good Weekend*. In it is an interview with Trish Goddard, and doesn't the hostess of the *7.30 Report* give Australia a nice slagging?

Apart from roasting just about everything about the place, she says: 'Australia is the most racist country in the world'. I found this particular statement curious, to say the least.

I looked out the brasco window and I'm buggered if I could see the Ku Klux Klan dynamiting churches and burning crosses in people's front yards.

I couldn't see any groups of people marching up the street wearing swastika armbands and chanting Nazi slogans and wanting to burn down synagogues or murder Jews.

And I can tell you I don't know of one beach or swimming pool where any people are barred because of the colour of their skin.

But according to Trish, Australia is the most racist country in the world.

Well, if so, why would she want to raise a child here?

I'm a racist myself. I know I am because I'm proud of my country. I'm a white Australian, and I have an Anglo-Saxon name, therefore — according to people like Al Grassby, some bleeding hearts in the media and the people at the *#?@ racial discrimination board who have to foster trouble and dissension to keep their jobs going — I automatically must be a racist. So rather than argue with these people, I'll take their word for it … even though I do try to help the full-blooded Aboriginal people in my third book.

'Boo, hoo, hoo!' sniffs Trish. 'I was in a bus and the children stared at me and one pulled my hair.'

Well, if you want to get around with your hair looking like someone's Araldited 200 char-grilled Gippsland worms on your head, what do you expect? Big bloody deal.

She then goes on to say: 'Australians better get used to not seeing blonde hair and blue eyes in the future' and 'I'm not just another pretty black face'.

I wonder when Ms Goddard first discovered she was so beautiful? She's got piggy eyes, a mouth like a Murray cod, and if anyone has ever the misfortune to see her standing up, she's got a backside big enough to sell advertising on. I'd like to know what brand of mirror she uses — I'll put one in every room in my house.

I might be a racist, but I'm definitely not a narcissist. But apart from Ms Goddard's blatant narcissism, let's have a look at her form as a hostess on a prime-time TV news show.

I think the kindest thing one could say about Trish as a newsreader is she has a nice smile: that's it.

Apart from Porky Pig, I've never heard anyone come up with so many malapropisms in my life: Wollongong becomes Wyalong; some bloke called Dr Herman became Dr Hormone till he eventually became Dr Herman Hormone; a book called *About Face* came out as *About Faced*.

I was also under the impression TV news presenters were supposed to do interviews, like Jana Wendt. I haven't seen Trish Goddard interview so much as the local dog-catcher.

Ironically, the only person she ever did interview was the alleged arch-villain of racism, Ron Casey.

I have to admit I never saw the interview, but they tell me it was as intellectually stimulating and philosophically meaningful as Ma Kettle interviewing Yogi Bear.

One could be cynical here, like a lot of others, and say that the only reason Trish Goddard got the job was so the ABC could appease all the whingeing feminists that work there, and show the world that it's neither sexist nor racist. In that case, why not use Justine Saunders or Lydia Miller, two proud and very attractive Aboriginal women?

I'm certain they could have performed the job just as well, and even pulled off the odd interview now and again … and without having to spend enough money every week doing up their hair to feed about 20 black kids starving in the Sudan.

But I'm not really a cynic. I'm merely a failed optimist.

We get more than a fair slathering of anti-racism and anti-apartheid now Ms Goddard has taken over the *7.30 Report*.

Well, maybe Ms Goddard could clear up a few points for me: Why is it a coloured person can wear a T-shirt with 'Black is Beautiful' printed on the front, yet if I wear one with 'White is Wonderful' on it I can be arrested for being a racist?

Some black lawyer in England put up a terrific stink about the term 'blackmail'.

It was the most offensive and racist term he'd ever come across, he screamed.

Yet the ANC, the African National Congress, has a blacklist — their term — of all the sportsmen and women that have competed in South Africa.

They're not a bad bunch of chaps in the ANC either.

Apart from letting off bombs in shopping centres, they have a real lot of love for their black brothers and sisters. Anyone they don't like they kill by tying their hands behind their backs and placing a tyre full of burning petrol around their necks.

It's called 'necklacing'.

So much for your black brothers and sisters, and our government gives them money.

Then a month or two ago there were all those Chinese students at Beijing University.

They beat up all the black students studying at the university, stole all their belongings then chased them to the airport and out of the country shouting 'kill the black devils'.

These are the same students we're giving political asylum to.

Maybe Ms Goddard might like to enrol in Beijing University and further her studies.

Then she might think twice before slagging a country that pays a whingeing Pommy ingrate $100,000 a year for doing virtually bugger all.

Then again, looking out my brasco window at the country I happen to be very fond of, I could be a bit biased and blinkered in my views, and perhaps Trish Goddard is right.

This is the most racist country in the world — all the men are racist, and the women are all hedonistic frumps, and maybe Australia is just a bastard of a place all round.

But if so, why would you want to raise another one here?

POOFS on PARADE

Compared with life in the city, living in the country can at times have its disadvantages.

There's the heat, the flies, the tyranny of distance, I suppose, and employment can be a bit hard to find.

Then, on the other hand, the air's cleaner, you can go out and leave your door unlocked, a friend in the country is a friend indeed and, for some unknown reason, beer in a country pub always tastes 10 times better than beer in a city hotel.

One definite thing about living in the country as opposed to living in Sydney is that the people in the bush don't have to put up with that annual, boring parade of sordid exhibitionism, the Gay Mardi Gras.

To tell you the truth, I'm even wondering why I'm bothering to write about this asinine assemblage of arseholes. But a couple of things in the news lately have brought it to mind.

Some mob of horses' hoofs in San Francisco calling themselves GRINCH (Gay Retaliation for Inexcusable

Negligence and Criminal Homophobia) is planning to stink-bomb department stores, stuff up airline flights, block traffic etc. around Christmas.

They want to bring more attention to the AIDS epidemic.

Look, blind Freddy knows the surest way to get AIDS is to be a junkie or a doughnut-puncher. Why these dag rattlers have to blame heterosexuals, and anybody else that can't condone their lifestyle or feel over-sorry for the predicament they've got themselves in and are spreading throughout the community, is beyond me.

Don't cop it up the date and you won't get AIDS — it's as simple as that. But leave the rest of us alone for Christ's sake and stop blaming everybody else.

The other thing that caught me eye was our old mate, fearless Fred Nile. Fred assembled his flock of holy rollers and bible-bashers from the Call To Australia party and, armed with the good book and singing hymns, off they marched along Oxford Street, taking the route of the Gay Mardi Gras and the battle right into the enemy's camp.

I thought this was hilarious, and on this occasion I have to give Fred and the Christians 10 points for ticker.

Not that I'm a fan of Fred Nile. Fred's dirty on the world, especially sex of any description.

I pondered on this until I tried to imagine Fred's missus, Elaine, in a gymslip or fellow Call To Australia pollie Marie Bignold in a suspender belt and fish-net stockings. God, if Fred has his way, women would need a prescription to buy a bra and men would still have to wear their Reg Grundys when taking a shower or having a crap.

And it wasn't all that long ago that zealots like Fred were burning people at the stake for talking in their sleep or laughing on Sunday, believing them to be possessed by the devil.

Anyway, off they marched, Fred and his gang, and didn't the poofs and the dykes get the hump? They jostled and abused the marchers, threw condoms full of urine, rubbish and other things at them, screamed obscenities and threatened Fred and his faithful followers with all manner of dreadful things.

Ironically, if the gays had been marching and you or I had taken the same action, we'd have been arrested for discrimination against homosexuals. But that's just part of the double standards we poor, silly straights are forced to live under in this State.

Anyway, despite the harassment, Fred and his gang made it to Taylor Square where they got up on a stage for a bit of eye rolling, breast beating, teeth gnashing and hymn singing.

Some skinny little poof jumped up, grabbed the microphone and trilled: 'Gay love is best, gay love is best'.

Well, I don't really know about this. Never having sodomised any of the blokes I have a drink with, I can't make a comparison either.

I'm just a straight, a square. I've spoken to a few girls who said they tried lesbianism, and all it did was leave a nasty taste in their mouths. But the young gentleman in question seemed quite sincere, so I shall give him the benefit of the doubt.

But fair dinkum, if you've seen one Gay Mardi Gras, you've seen the lot.

It's a drag and a pain in the arse — and I don't mean that as a pun.

It's the same thing every year.

Squads of simpering, sniggering men pushing floats, either dressed up as fairies or done up in sequin G-strings flashing their hairy bums to the multitude.

And believe me, if you've seen one bloke's hairy khyber, you've seen them all. They're not very appetising. I was forced to look at mine in the mirror once when I had to pull a tick out of it, and I wasn't turned on by the sight of my hairy blurter.

Other blokes' turn me on even less, especially ones that have been punched around the ring more times than Mike Tyson's sparring partners.

The poofs' other thrill seems to be getting dressed up as nuns and slagging the church. I suppose slagging religion could be construed as funny, but when I think of nuns, I think of one who is dying in India — Mother Theresa. She spent her life helping the underprivileged and the lepers.

Personally, I wouldn't swap one Mother Theresa for a thousand of those dills from the strip who kiss each other and flash their dates to the crowd.

But if you've ever met any of the mob from Oxford Street, they're oh-so-hip. They've been there, done that, and everybody else is prosaic and mundane.

Well I reckon their Mardi Gras is passé and boring. So why not liven it up?

Instead of slagging the church and nuns all the time, why not have a go at the Muslims? They hate poofters. Abou el Moundhir in Algeria cuts their throats on sight. Death to the poofters. Organise a few floats rubbishing Islam. Leave the nun's habits and priest's collars at home. Get done up as mullahs or wear kaftans with the backs cut away and have their hairy quoits sticking out of those. But make sure you let all the blokes with the bushy, black moustaches who visit the mosque at Lakemba in on the joke too. Then we would all see a gay old time at the Mardi Gras.

There would be lumps of lesbians and pieces of poofs scattered from one end of Oxford Street to the other. At least the taxpayers would be getting some value for the half million dollars or so the government give the gay community for putting it on.

Oh, and if any queens read this and claim I'm poofter bashing, check out one of the blokes I dedicated my latest book to. He made a great contribution to Australia and didn't waste his life flashing his bum around Oxford Street.

TALL poppies deserve SHORT SHRIFT

There's this thing in Australia they keep talking about called the tall poppy syndrome.

You become very successful in your field or make a lot of money and supposedly jealous people, who have either got or done nothing themselves, knock your efforts and can't wait to see you go bad.

Even a lowlife like me gets it occasionally to some degree, mainly from dopey sheilas who are frustrated writers.

They're convinced I'm a millionaire and it burns their arses to think that a wombat like me can be a successful writer while they, through absolutely no fault of their own and any lack of talent, can't quite seem to get it together.

So they come out with the sarcastic remarks and snide innuendoes.

If they had half a brain in their heads and approached me with a little civility instead of trying to show me how clever they are, I'd only be too happy to help them as best I could.

Instead, I feel like pissing on them from a great height. But this tall poppy syndrome still intrigues me.

It's almost as if we're supposed to worship people with money or position. Not that for an instant I'm against making a buck.

If by some strange quirk of fate my books started to take off overseas I'd be straight down to buy a new car tomorrow; I don't think I've ever driven one let alone owned one.

I'd probably buy a bit of property up the North Coast, then a boat and then do some travelling.

I'm in no way against making money. But I detest the vulgarity of wealth. I call it 'the short daisy syndrome'.

The tall poppy syndrome in reverse. How many people do you know with money that are totally convinced their crap doesn't stink and everybody's a mug bar them?

One minute they've got the arse out of their pants getting around in old bangers. The next time you see them they're driving red Mercs, wearing Gucci leather and with enough gold chains round them to sink a Manly ferry.

Eastern suburbs real estate salesmen, advertising yuppies and some drug dealers I have met slip easily into this category. But two particular high-flying tall poppies have been in the news lately: Alan Bond and Christopher Skase. So I thought I might take a look at them and the vulgarity of their wealth.

Take Alan Bond. A little, fat demigod in a pinstripe suit surrounded by 'yes' men. Not all of them yes men. If Alan said 'no' they'd say no too.

He's supposed to be a hot-shot wheeler-dealer yet he's in all sorts of strife. So he won the America's Cup a few years back — blowing millions on a giant ego trip. Big bloody deal.

The Seppos got it straight back and where is it now? The Kiwis have got it in a milk shed somewhere in the North Island. And the Yanks are about to get it straight back off them.

Frank Hardy summed up the America's Cup in a few succinct words: 'The new rich, fighting the old rich, and boring the tits off the poor.'

Bond paid $50 million for Van Gogh's *Irises* — another ego trip to hang on his wall. Then we find out it's half in hock to Sotheby's in London, and now they want it back. What a load of crap!

Then there's the coiffed and groomed Christopher Skase and the lovely Trixie or Dixie or whatever her name is.

Like Bond he's borrowed to the hilt overseas, upsetting our balance of payments even more. Now to get himself out of hock he's going to flog off his resorts to the kindly Japanese.

Then you find out the Queensland National Party has $50 million invested in Skase's Qintex. Pooh. Even the mention of this bunch makes you immediately reach for the can of Glen–20.

The way they make their money bugs me even more. You never hear of Bond or Skase starting up a factory to recycle waste paper and help save our dwindling forests.

They wouldn't put money into researching a new, environmentally safe motor or finance some scientists to find a way of eradicating industrial pollution. No, destroy a rainforest and put in a pulp mill or a petro-chemical complex. Bulldoze a wetland or a mangrove forest and build another resort, complete with giant swimming pools and artificial waterfalls. A plastic imitation of Babylon for the overseas rich.

But the vulgarity of their wealth is what really gives me the hump. Alan Bond spent a million dollars on his kid's wedding: flying in guests, hangers-on, lobster and champagne to Perth from all over Australia.

Skase bulldozed three huge, old houses in Brisbane to build just one for the lovely Trixie or Dixie or whatever her name is and himself.

Bond has got a 50-metre cruiser. Skase has a 33-metre one.

Skase is the darling of the Brisbane social set, according to one gushing social cockroach who writes for one of the Brisbane papers.

If Skase is so smart and so popular why doesn't he put the snip on some of the fleas who come to his parties for a grand or two? Hah! These people wouldn't give you the steam off their turds.

Eileen Bond spends more than 100 workers would earn in a lifetime throwing the same sort of parties. For what? So Trixie or Dixie or whatever her name is and Alan and Christopher can stand round in their evening gowns and tuxedos getting their rocks off out of a lot of social cockroaches dagging them.

These people are supposed to be icons of Australian business, and if you knock them in any way it's the tall poppy syndrome and you're a nark.

But look at it this way. If Alan Bond and the rest of those ego-tripping Perth millionaires hadn't wasted their time with the America's Cup, Ralph Sarich would probably still be in Australia building his orbital engines.

If Christopher Skase had bulldozed only one house instead of three to build his mansion we'd probably have a treatment for multiple sclerosis.

If Alan Bond hadn't bought *Irises* we'd more than likely have a cure for cancer.

But then why bother with mundane things for the short daisies when you can build monuments to your ego and be Jack The Lad in front of a horde of gushing sycophants?

BARRETT'S gone A-PUNTING

How do you know when you're a fair dinkum Australian? I reckon it's when people who don't know your address can contact you at your local TAB.

When you walk into the TAB and the manager says there's a letter for you, I reckon you're dead set, one of the boys. You're true blue.

I got a letter at the TAB the other week. From Lancashire, England. And, from of all blokes, John Monie, the ex-Parramatta football coach.

He said he liked my first book. It reminded him of home. He missed Terrigal but England was still good and the locals were looking after him.

It was a good letter all round and I replied immediately because John Monie's a real good bloke. Except for one thing. His @!%#*#! tips.

I met John Monie at the Terrigal TAB and good bloke or not, it was one of the worst things I ever did in my life.

You see, I love a bet and so does John and every time he'd see me he always seemed to have one going. If not him it was 'Sterlo' (Peter Sterling) or 'The Crow' (Mick Cronin) or he got the whisper from the team masseur whose brother was the trainer. And what could a mug punter like me do but bow to better judgment?

Now I admit, when it comes to picking winners, I couldn't tip water out of my shoe. But fair dinkum, Monie gave me more bad tips than a box full of rotten asparagus.

Yet every time I'd walk into the TAB there would be Monie and his brother stuffing all the chops in their kicks saying they had one going at Kembla or Werribee and giving me that old surfie line: 'You should have been here earlier.'

Another interesting person I met at Terrigal TAB was Frank Hardy. He was renting a place at the time not far from mine while working on a play.

I spotted him out of the corner of my eye and thought, 'Hey, that's bloody Frank Hardy the author'.

I wanted to meet him because even though he's reputed to be an old commo and a bit of a lemon, he's still the man who wrote *Power Without Glory*, the Australian classic.

Ever met Frank Hardy? A complete stranger going up to or approaching Frank is like stepping into someone's backyard and they've got one of those bull-necked, blue heeler cattle dogs tied up in there. It's been kicked and starved and the kids across the road have been throwing rocks at it. The day you walk in it's just broken its chain.

'Excuse me,' I said politely. 'Are you Mr Hardy the writer?'

'Grrrowrr! Arrggh! Rowf, rowf, snarl, grrrr!'

'I read *Power Without Glory* and saw it on the ABC. It was great.'

'Snarl, snark, arrggh! Rowf, rowf, grrrrr, arrgh! Rowf, rowf, aaarrrggghhh!'

'Well, thanks Mr Hardy. It's been nice talking to you. I'll see you later.'

I left after my first encounter with Frank Hardy minus the backside out of my jeans, part of my arm missing and needing about 25 stitches in my arse. But it wasn't just me.

Frank and his pipe had just about everybody in the TAB, including the staff, terrified. He was a monster. He'd stuff up bets, get there late for races, lose his tickets and it was everybody's fault but his own.

One thing I did notice; the bastard used to win a lot more money than me. I played Frank pretty wide.

Then one day, completely out of the blue, Frank was nice to me. He walked up to me and said, 'I didn't know you were an actor.'

Well, I'm not. But I can run half a dozen words together and now and again I get a run in a soapie or something — generally as a heavy, a moron or a drunk in a pub.

'I saw you in *The Lizard King* on the ABC the other night,' he said. 'You were very good.'

I thought, Frank's definitely putting something in that pipe besides Dutch Old Flake. Then I remembered the show and how Frank was now into writing plays.

I had a few lines as a grazier called Forhay, running around in an Akubra hat, moleskins and R.M. Williams boots.

Anyway, Frank must have figured I was a bit of an artsy-fartsy actor and he was almost civil to me after that. But actor, writer or whatever, both he and Monie were convinced I was a definite mug punter and treated me accordingly.

But I got even on both the bastards one day. I kicked their arses from one end of the TAB to the other.

It was a Brisbane meeting and a horse called In The Limelight. I don't know how I picked it and there was a 5/2-on favourite in the race.

It was like a voice from the heavens saying: 'Bob, they're gonna pull the favourite up. Go for the lightweight with the Sydney jockey.' I'd just fluked a quinella, so I had plenty to throw on it.

Monie asked me what I'd backed and when he saw what it was paying on the teletext he sniggered louder than ever.

I even tried to tell Frank I thought it was a good thing. He saw the teletext, looked at me like I was something left over from a garbage strike and, after almost suffocating me in a cloud of pipe smoke, went back to abusing the staff.

Monie was sitting next to me and Frank was right in front of the TV when the favourite dropped dead and In The Limelight came off the rails to win by almost two lengths. It paid $54 for a win and $9 for a place. And that's gospel.

Frank almost swallowed his pipe. Monie looked at me like I was the Messiah.

I had $50 bills coming out my ears. I was in that good a mood I even shouted John lunch. As we were marching up Campbell Crescent, like two grenadier guards, I spotted Frank getting into his car and he looked at me across the roof, shook his head and smiled.

It was a big day for me I can tell you.

I'm certain it was the first time I've ever shouted anyone lunch in my life. And it was definitely the first time I've ever seen Frank Hardy smile.

THE Wellington's ON THE OTHER FOOT

Less enlightened women who read my column could possibly misconstrue it at times as being sexist or chauvinistic.

Not really. It's just that at times, I don't believe this equality of the sexes is 100 per cent correct.

One thing I do share with women, however, is an abhorrence of rape or violent sexual abuse. I think any man who rapes a woman should be gaoled.

And as for those creatures involved in crimes like the Anita Cobby or Janine Balding cases — not only do I believe in capital punishment, I think they should be castrated then burnt at the stake.

But I'd like to report on two cases of sexual assault where charges were never laid. Perhaps they should've been.

The first involves a mate of mine, John, who works for an airline company.

He had an affair with a stewardess; let's call her Miss X.

After a while the affair soured. John wanted out. Miss X persisted.

Arguments and acrimony evolved.

They culminated in Miss X coming round to John's place one night half-drunk and carrying a bottle of wine and demanding to be let in: she was horny.

John told her to piss off. Miss X stood on his verandah abusing him so John went out to reason with her, got more abuse and hit over the head with the bottle for his trouble.

With Miss X still abusing him, John went inside to clean up the blood and, rather than be a cad and belt her in the mouth, he called the police.

When the desk sergeant asked how many men there were and John replied 'one woman', he laughed.

By the time they got there, Miss X had decamped and the police, who were less than amused at John's story, were seriously thinking of booking him for causing a public mischief.

The next case concerns yours truly — balding, overweight hack writer R.G. Barrett.

Before the nice people moved in next door, the house was rented to a team of cretinous surfies downstairs and a bunch of half-baked, liberated women upstairs.

The liberated women didn't mind a drink or a party. A number of men and cars came and went. I'd say that, even though the girls were only rooting for their friends, in six months they never made an enemy in NSW.

When they found out I was a writer, single and presumably rich, they were always inviting me in for a drink. But I played them wide.

I knew once I started going into their place they'd be in mine and I'd never get them out.

The more they asked, the more I refused. Which really burnt their arses.

One in particular, not a bad sort but completely Yarramugundi, fancied me.

But still I kept my celibate resolve. A polite-but-firm no — even when she'd come knocking on my door smelling of Arpel and her tits bulging out of her tank top like Graham Kennedy's eyes.

Eventually I found out the new owners were moving in and the women were going, so rather than be a complete snob and a suspected poof I thought I'd go in. One night, with a few cans of beer, I did.

It was as I suspected. Dirty dishes everywhere and mould on the fridge. The conversation was reasonable but, all up, not my cup of tea.

I shared my beers and politely took my leave.

The nutter who fancied me said she'd walk me home.

To which I replied, it's only next door, I can catch a cab, don't worry about it.

She persisted and when we got to my front door she pounced. She literally kicked the door open, ripped off my gear, and hers, and bonked me on the loungeroom floor.

I barely had time to get over the first one when she gave me another serve, which went from the loungeroom to the front room.

I finally managed to get her out of the house but she returned, foaming at the mouth at seven the next morning.

After that it was on. I'd be laying back watching TV or reading a book and crash! Up would go the roller door in the garage and there would be Fatal Attractions, primed-up on flagon wine and ready for another six-rounder.

Now I don't mind a bit of the other. I love it. But not on Sunday afternoon during the semis. And definitely not right on half-time when Balmain and Manly are 16–all. Nor during *Dr Who* or *Minder.*

There was definitely no affection there, let alone any love, and it was just getting to be plain hard work.

I decided to break off the engagement. Christ! Talk about hell hath no fury. I thought for sure she was going to set fire to my house and in her myopic rage try to castrate poor old Beryl, the old tabby that hangs around my place thinking she's a tom.

Anyway they moved out and that was almost that.

The finale was me bumping into Fatal Attractions one night in a bar with two of her girlfriends: a couple of mealy-mouthed, post-graduate lesbians with a lot of hang-ups.

I didn't ignore her, but I certainly didn't lay out the welcome mat either.

She sooled the two girlfriends onto me and I copped their drinks over my head then Fatal Attractions kicked me in the nuts. I left.

The reason I'm writing this, however, is not to brag about myself or my mate John's sex life or the hypnotic effect we have over women.

What if the tables had been reversed? What if my mate John had gone round to Miss X's house demanding a wellington then, after getting knocked back, abused her and hit her over the head with a bottle?

He'd have got two years. And what about if I, after practically raping the girl next door, had repeatedly gone back to her house and forced her to have sex with me against her will then when she finally got rid of me I abused her in a bar and got two mates to throw beers over her and then I kicked her in the lamington?

Knowing my form, I'd have got 15 years.

But I never went to the police. Being old school, I'm not into shelving people.

I just accepted that this is more of the double standard we poor, heterosexual Aussie males are forced to live under. Perhaps I should've shelved them.

My life is ruined. What decent, self-respecting woman would want me now?

The POLITICS of POT

Somebody asked me the other day what I thought of the drug problem and the drug laws in NSW.

Well, someone a lot more upstanding in the community and a lot more intelligent than myself answered this for me.

A good man, Judge Rod Madgwick, had to sentence Christopher Withell of Kyogle, a citizen of good character according to his Honour, to three months in gaol and a three-year good behaviour bond for cultivation and possession of marijuana.

In reluctantly sentencing Withell, Madgwick said the law had to be respected 'even when the law is controversial, smacks of hypocrisy and when the judge himself believes the law ought to be changed'.

And he added his voice to those who believed it was time to review the law when it came to people caught in possession of marijuana.

Well, I don't know whether this will ruin my reputation or have me declared a communist radical or an enemy of the state, but I have to agree with Madgwick. In fact, I'll go one better and say that as far as I'm concerned the law stinks worse than lobster bait and so do some of the people making and enforcing it.

There's that much heroin, cocaine, speed and ecstasy around, it's cheaper than ever and the pushers will throw in a dozen green stamps and an electric toaster with every deal you buy. Yet you can't buy a bag of pot for love nor money.

The pushers are driving around in their Mercedes, with their gold chains, doing property deals and business as usual. Yet the only people being arrested are ordinary working people and a few hippies or alternative life-stylers living in the bush. Heroin addicts, whose only claim to fame is breaking into houses and bashing old ladies for their handbags, get free methadone, needles, money, and all the sympathy in the world.

Anyone caught with a bit of pot is hounded and sent to prison, where — with truth in sentencing, which is 25 years for having a milk crate in your garage — you're likely to finish up forever.

How about some truth in charging? I'll give you an idea of how an ordinary worker, a punter, can go down for a long stretch for committing no real crime at all.

You're a taxpayer with no criminal record. You hate heroin, the addicts and the dealers. You're not a rich yuppie and have no desire to be seen shoving coke up your nose. Nor are you a 250kg bikie revved up on speed roaring around on a Harley.

You like nothing more than a drink and a bit of a puff while you listen to Jimmy Barnes or The Mentals.

You're also sick of paying an arm and a leg for a smoke, if you can get it, so with a few seeds you've saved over the years, you decide to put a few plants in the backyard and have a free smoke.

The plants are coming along nicely, about 15cm high. Then along comes Operation Dob In Your Neighbour. NOAH. And one of those wonderful things, a concerned citizen, shelves you.

You're watching TV with the missus and kids one night and crash-bang on the door, it's the drug squad with guns out. They've more than likely brought the TRG or a SWOS group with them to give them something to do.

They tip your house upside down while the boys in the baseball caps poke their shotguns in the kids' faces. They find your five lousy plants and you're dragged off to the slammer and charged.

But you don't get charged with the five lousy plants. Oh no, that'd be no good on the charge sheets or for the government's statistics. The politicians have to look like they're doing something about the drug problem, don't they? You get charged with five plants at $5000 a plant, plus the 10 seeds you had left over with a projected street value of another $50,000. And you're up for drugs worth $75,000. A trafficable amount and an indictable offence.

Get a lemon for a police prosecutor and a beak a lot less enlightened than Rod Madgwick, and you're looking at five years, maybe more. For a charge of offending absolutely no-one and being caught with a few grams of weed that's unsmokeable.

And in all reality you shouldn't even be in court in the first place, and the cops should be out busting heroin and cocaine dealers and their addicts.

They're the ones breaking into houses, robbing banks and mugging old ladies.

Not only is this system of police and politicians juggling statistics disgraceful, it exacerbates the whole drug problem.

Look at it this way — I can't remember seeing a drug bust in the paper of less than half a million dollars in the past two years. No-one ever gets caught with a kilo of heroin, or two kilos of cocaine or pot. It's always $50 million worth of heroin,

$45 million worth of coke or marijuana plants worth $320 million. Write your own ticket and add the date.

And the media are as much to blame for this drug sensationalism. Idiots read all this. They see dollar signs in their empty heads and go off to get involved in drugs, thinking they've only got to make one good score and they're set for life. So more smack, hash and coke gets onto the streets for our kids.

Anyway, while you're enjoying the summer break think of Christopher Withell in gaol for doing sweet bugger all. According to the court transcripts, 'He had no commercial motivation at all. Never profited out of the drug and had been growing it for his own use and occasionally to share with friends.'

Not a bad bust for the police and not a bad statistic for the government. Not quite as good as that one in Wollongong where they arrested a paraplegic woman for having two hemp plants in her backyard. But a good one all the same.

PUBLIC Dis-service

Any coalminers, shearers, workers on building sites out there? Nurses and interns working 20-hour shifts in hospitals or even those who haven't got a job?

I want you all to spare a thought for our poor, beleaguered NSW public servants.

I can remember encountering this thing called the 'public service mentality' on one particular occasion — very vividly.

About five years ago a couple of mates of mine, whom I'll call Joe and Barry, and I did a TV commercial for which we were paid $250. Not one of those glamorous Arpel or Cointreau ads. This was for the NSW Anti-Litter Campaign — *Do The Right Thing*.

We were three garbos hanging off the back of a garbage truck. I was the 'hero' and had to run behind the truck in my stubbies with a snot-rag jammed on my head, pick up a milk carton and toss it in the scoop. After about three hours of me falling in and out of the scoop, getting covered in crap and dirt, we got it shot. And I don't care what you say, 250 bananas for three hours of stuffing around isn't bad dough.

The best part, however, was we did it in North Sydney and we took a huge Esky full of icy cold beers with us. Then after it was over we went down to Berry's Bay where another mate, Terry, had a yacht he'd built and we spent the rest of the afternoon sailing around the harbour; four old mates getting pissed and telling each other what good blokes we were.

The following Friday night we were in a hotel talking about what a good time we'd had. We weren't even discussing the money, just what a top day it had been all round. Standing with us was another friend Paul, a public servant who's been with the water board since he left school and is now a grade 15 minor flunky of some description.

Paul's been at his desk job that long now his ears droop down around his elbows. He's also one of those types who doesn't like to think somebody's done or got something better than him. He listened to our little story with disdain, then said contemptuously: 'Well, I might not be in the same league as you movie stars. But all I know is I have to go to work tomorrow morning (Saturday) and get $168 to sit on my arse for three hours and do nothing.'

Well, bully for you we thought. If you can bludge 168 bucks of taxpayers' money for three hours of sitting on your arse and get away with it, half your luck. But I don't think I'd brag about it.

About two weeks later I walked into a different hotel. Paul was there with Terry who had a look of mild disbelief. Paul still had his one of smug conceit.

'What's going on?' I asked.

Terry shook his head and pointed at Paul. 'Ask him.'

'What's up Paul?' I asked.

'We're on strike,' was the curt reply.

Hello, I mused to myself. A public servant on strike. What could he possibly be on strike for? The tea lady brought ginger snaps instead of iced vo-vos? There had to be a reason.

'What are you on strike for?' I asked.

Paul didn't blink and looked me straight in the eye. 'More wages and better conditions,' he said.

It's five years down the track and I'm still trying to figure this one out. How can you stand up in a pub and state what a well-paid bludge your job is, then a fortnight later go on strike for more money and better conditions? Could somebody explain it to me? Or is this just part of that phenomenon called 'the public service mentality'? Well, if it is, I think Australia's in a lot of trouble.

TAKE Derryn Hinch... PLEASE

I was with some blokes in a pub the other day engaged in deep conversation; discussing the sort of things the intelligentsia of Australia are apt to discuss in public bars.

Football, racing, boxing, advanced calculus, autogenic-visualisation, Einstein's theory of relativity. Somehow the subject got round to Derryn Hinch.

The change in mood was almost electrifying and you should have heard some of the things these blokes said about Hinch.

It started with the usual derogatory remarks. He was a scumbag, a hairbag, a toe-rag, a boil on the arse of society. He had a grease-trap for a mind. His face looked like a cross between a rat hiding behind a broom and the rear view of someone having a crap over a hedge. He was so miserable even his shadow keeps as far away from him as possible. Terrible things.

And as my companions got drunker they got worse.

One bloke reckoned he was the sootikin that fell out of mother nature's vagina. Another bloke said his dog had more taste when it licked its nuts than Hinch ever had.

Then my friends turned and asked me what I thought of Derryn Hinch.

What could I say? I simply shrugged and said I didn't mind him. Well, talk about almost cause a riot. I thought these blokes were going to chase me out of the pub with broomsticks.

But it's true. I admit I loathed him at first. But now I find I don't mind the tedious, loathsome little centipede. In fact, for some reasons I actually admire him.

Okay, he's a hanging judge I admit. And I don't agree with him that convicted shoplifters should have their hands cut off.

Nor do I think we should have public beheadings for people found with smooth tyres on their cars.

I'm not sure about his views on capital punishment, though I would like to see that creep responsible for the Hoddle Street massacre put in front of a firing squad and see how he likes being shot himself.

But if Hinch goes for the throat on paedophiles, that's okay by me. These repulsive creatures deserve no mercy and should be named and exposed. Along with drug dealers, Asians with smack and Colombians with coke.

Even though I, like a lot of others, have been done for low-range DUI, I agree with him about drunken drivers and his shame file.

People who drink 20 schooners or a bottle of whisky then get behind the wheel of a car and kill some poor unfortunate are no better than murderers and should be treated as such.

And when some ethnic groups get caught pulling an insurance rort Hinch gets in and names them, unlike the other media nancy boys who are terrified to tell the truth lest some bleeding heart might call them a racist.

Derryn is also a true blue greenie. He exposes those toxic waste dumpers and he fights for our rainforests and oceans, naming the Japanese for what they are — environmental rapists.

And I give Hinch top marks for going into bat for those beaut schoolkids on the South Coast who succeeded in stopping some idiot of a mayor and a bunch of moronic council workers from needlessly killing several families of brushtail possums living harmlessly in an old tree in a park.

I feed a bunch of possums on my sun deck and I think they're about the most laughable little critters going.

Like Hinch, I detest people that are cruel to our dwindling wildlife. Especially some of these so-called 'sports shooters' who can't wait to get half-full of piss, grab a rifle and go out and shoot anything that moves. Not rabbits, feral cats or pigs and dogs. Anything that moves. The idiots.

But there's one thing I really admire Derryn Hinch for. He's a tit man. I don't mind a good set of boobs. And evidently neither does Derryn. If you need proof of this, get some photos of his ex-fiancée Lynda Stoner. You wouldn't find a bigger pair of maracas anywhere in Australia. They're rippers.

If you had one of those filled with Jack Daniels and the other with Bundy you could just about stay drunk for the rest of your life.

And what about his missus, actress Jacki Weaver. She's not badly stacked herself. Get hold of a video of a movie called *Stork*. Jacki drops her gazonkas out in one scene and there's nothing wrong with her pantry shelf I can tell you. The movie's getting a bit old, but I reckon they'd be holding up okay.

So say what you like about Derryn Hinch. Call him an obnoxious, execrable little toad if you will. Say he's the kind of person that would give a coprophile a bad taste in his mouth. Call him a frustrated parking cop. Say he goes through life like an untipped waiter. He'd make an ideal perfect stranger. He thinks people worship the ground he's just crawled across. He's that miserable you couldn't warm up to him if you were cremated with him. He gets up on the wrong side of the floor every morning. The only thing that keeps growing on him without nourishment is his ego. Go ahead. Say what you will.

But I reckon anybody that's environmentally aware, hates child molesters and likes big tits, can't be all bad.

It's time to MUNCH our MOGGIES

My old moggie Achmet has snuffed it. I got up and there he was underneath the car in the driveway dead as a roll-mop.

I don't know what he died of but it definitely wasn't hard work or over-exercise. Achmet had the best lifestyle of any cat going around. All he did was eat, sleep, lay in the long grass and chase the occasional lizard.

Nine years I had the old bludger. He was a good mate and, living the hermit's existence I do, he was one of the only mates I had. He was a good bloke and I'll miss him, both me and his tortoiseshell girlfriend, Beryl, from up the road.

And if I were to say I didn't shed a tear or two when I prepared Achmet for life's big journey I would be telling a lie. RIP Achmet. You were a good mate and I loved you.

Anyway, as I was out there in the backyard, beneath the leaden skies, lowering Achmet into the cold, cold ground, a couple of thoughts occurred to me.

What about all these so-called animal lovers who get pets on a whim, keep them for a while then when they're sick of them dump them out at the RSPCA to be put down? Did you know that, according to the RSPCA, in the next 10 years 2.75 million pets will be destroyed throughout Australia? And in the past 45 years the RSPCA has had to slaughter almost 20 million cats and dogs? That's sick.

There are trendies out there, mainly in the cities, who buy dogs as a fashion whim or a status symbol. I can see their point though. What could be trendier than to be seen strolling the streets of Paddington in a nice new, blue and grey Ca Va tracksuit with a matching Weimaraner?

Or how absolutely so with-it to be spotted parking your iridescent brown Nissan 4WD on the footpath (that's what 4WD cars are used for in the city) then alighting in a beige Kelvin Kline windcheater with two matching Afghans? Or how simply marvellous to be noticed in a Double Bay or Toorak coffee shop in a fur coat with a nicely contrasting pair of French poodles?

I've even heard of women pissing off their dogs and cats when they get a new lounge because the poor bloody things don't match the colour. You wonder how these arseholes live with themselves.

Then, as I sent Achmet to that great box of Whiskettes in the sky, another thought struck me. Even though my heart's breaking I'm still on the lookout for an earner. What happens to all those skins and meat?

There's a bloody fortune in pelts going to waste out there. And the first half-smart business man/woman who doesn't mind getting a bit of dirt on their hands is going to make a bomb.

I've worked boning kangaroos and helped to skin them — doing dogs and cats couldn't be any worse. It'd be a doddle.

Work it out. The RSPCA bowls over around 4000 cats and dogs a week. Think how many jackets, hats and gloves that would make? I'm fair dinkum. There are rich Seppos and Japs with more money than brains who would pay a fortune for a padded jacket made out of red cattle dog or blue heeler.

How about a nice double-breasted number with full collar made from Australian leather and inlaid with strips of cross kelpie labrador? These designer clothes would be the talk of Tokyo and Fifth Avenue.

One-upmanship is all these mugs are after. Imagine Jane Fonda doing her workout on TV in a pair of Down Under brand Rottweiler leg warmers. She'd be a sensation. G-strings for all those poofs in San Francisco made out of silky terriers. Wouldn't that tickle their fancies?

Then there's all that lovely, juicy, tender meat. They eat cats in certain parts of China and the Koreans would walk barefoot across broken glass for a cheap feed of dog meat.

Some people with racist tendencies pooh-pooh the Koreans for eating dogs. But why shouldn't they? Isn't this all part of this multiculturalism thing we're supposed to cop whether we like it or not? To deny these potential customers a nice feed of cat or dog is tantamount to vile, wretched racism. If they want to eat cats and dogs good luck to them.

Crispy skin Australian moggie; sounds all right to me. It could be the new taste sensation to sweep China. And imagine those Koreans ripping into a plate of gom luk cross-bred bull terrier kelpie in red bean sauce. I can see them drooling now.

So, though it pained me deeply to see my old mate Achmet toss tails, some good did come out of it. If ever I had the money I'd look into this — 2.75 million skins ain't as crazy as you think. Divide that in half and that's how many jackets you get at around $500 each. Plus the meat, at say $30 a kilo, and you'd watch the cash roll in.

A PLAGUE on PUFFERS

I imagine I won't win too many friends with this week's column because, from what I can see, they're all pretty keen puffers at *People*.

However, cigarette smoking has well and truly been in the news lately. Surgeons are refusing to operate on cigarette smokers.

So I thought I might butt in too, so to speak.

Firstly, I don't smoke cigarettes and I hate the stinkin' bloody things. But I used to. Yes, I am an ex-smoker.

I can still remember my times as a smoker.

I first started when I was at school. I wanted to look tough without getting a tattoo and I also wanted to look like my idol of the time, James Dean.

So, along with two or three other young flips at Randwick Boys' High, I used to sneak into the toilets and have a puff.

I also used to like to have one hanging out the corner of my mouth when I was playing snooker.

However, I used to get asthma at the time and the doctor I was sent to told me bluntly he was wasting his time and mine if I continued smoking.

So instead of whingeing about him discriminating against me I tipped half a packet of dotches down the toilet and got rid of my asthma.

I know I didn't smoke any of those nancy-boy filter tip things though.

I was a full-on, bad arse macho man: Lucky Strike, Chesterfield, Camel, Pall Mall etc.

Somehow, I must have got sick of waking up coughing, with my mouth tasting like a sumo wrestler had crapped in it, so I stopped and never smoked again. Except once. I had a couple in a gaol cell one night.

Personally I don't give a rat's arse if people want to smoke.

If they're silly enough to pay heaps for something that stuffs up their health they're entitled to put it to good use.

There are places to smoke and as far as I'm concerned, while they are in their own homes, they can fill a bucket full of cigarettes, toss in some petrol, light it and stick their heads in the bucket.

I just wish smokers would stop whingeing about their rights and see themselves for the grubs they are.

Have a look at a bus stop or a seat on a railway station next time you pass one.

All around it will be squashed butts, matches and gobs of phlegm. All for someone else to clean up.

I often catch a train down from Gosford to Sydney which generally has two smoking cars on it. Each one smells like a public toilet in Bombay.

However, the smokers still have to sneak to the rear of the non-smoking cars and light up; not worrying about the fumes still drifting in.

At the end of the trip the rear of the carriage is littered with butts, matches, more gollys and empty beer cans.

Once again, all for some poor mug to clean up. They're pigs. No, not pigs. I've never seen a pig yet with a fag hanging out of its mouth.

The mentality of smokers never ceases to amaze me either.

They're either as thick as half-baked damper or super-belligerent.

I've been studying the form at the TAB. Someone blows a big cloud of rotten smoke all over you and when you wave the crap away with your ticket they glare at you as if you just called their mother a whore.

Smokers are always going on about their rights. And they do have rights. They've got a right to give themselves emphysema, lung cancer, asthma, high blood pressure, bronchitis, rotten breath, yellow teeth, stuffed-up taste buds, among myriad other things.

But enjoyable as all these things are, they don't have a right to share them with everyone else.

What right did that arsehole in London have to toss his cigarette butt in the Underground and cause a fire that killed 50 people?

What right did that goose have to start a fire with his cigarette in that backpackers' hotel in Kings Cross and kill all those poor, battling bloody tourists?

What right do wallies have to flick their lighted butts out of car windows and possibly start a bushfire which could kill people, the wildlife and wipe out half the surrounding countryside?

I look at cigarettes this way. I can go half the day without something to eat. I can go half the week without a drink. I can go for hours without having a crap. And being a bachelor with not the best scone in the world I can go for a fair while without having a root.

But ask a smoker to go for a couple of hours without a cigarette, like on a train or a plane, and they scream.

No wonder the tobacco companies are laughing all the way to the bank.

TV ADS... the REAL THING???

Love them or loathe them, television commercials are here to stay. Some I don't mind. Others make me want to throw up.

I think the 'Don't wrap it. Post-pak it' ad for the post office is good for a chuckle. And those 'Oils ain't oils, Sol' commercials always make me laugh. And I love that sheila with the towel on her head who comes on just after the news spieling about her Dishlex dishwasher.

I can't stand that bloody Mrs Marsh and her Colgate fluoride tooth tougheners. And I'd willingly take an RPG-7 to Rosie and her yuppie boyfriend in the back of that limousine talking about the *Financial Review*. 'You really nailed 'em that time, Rosie.' I'd nail them — and the driver.

I'd do the same with an M-60 to all those bony, bored-looking models in those French perfume and trendy liqueur ads. They stand there as if someone's waving a piece of rotten fish under their noses and look like a good root and a green apple would kill the lot of them.

But if there's one ad I can't stand, one that really makes me want to slash my wrists and swallow a can of Drano, it's one of those Resch's ads. 'The beer we drink round here.'

It shows these two trendies with their luggage and a guitar getting off a train at some heat-scorched, desolate station in the bush. Up bowls this boofheaded cow-cocky in a battered Akubra and R.M. Williams boots to pick them up in an old Holden ute.

As the laconic-looking cocky squints through the heat haze and wipes the sweat from his brow, one of the trendies, tossing his gear in the ute, says: 'It's hot.'

And the cow-cocky nods and says: 'Yeah. It's been a scorcher. But I got a cold one waiting for you back at the house.'

The little group then goes back to a huge old country house to be met by more trendies and a couple of good sorts. Then they all proceed to pour gallons of Resch's down their parched throats. The trendies make out with the good sorts. The cow-cocky gets to talk to the dog.

The main reason I hate this ad is because the cow-cocky driving the ute and complaining about the heat is me. And if you were curious about some of the bollocks that goes on in the glitzy, glamour world of TV commercials, this is a prime example.

It's a scorcher eh! We shot the thing in the middle of winter and I was half dead with the flu. The shoot was supposed to take two days but we spent a week huddled under blankets, freezing our rings off on the verandah of some old deserted house for sale out past Windsor, NSW.

It rained every day on what was supposed to be a shot of the evening summer sun going down over the paddocks and trees. The director was pulling his hair out by the roots; I couldn't stop sneezing.

Finally the sun came out for about an hour so we all got in front of the camera and poured hundreds of cans of Resch's mixed with soda water down our screeches and tried to look as if we were enjoying every drop of it.

Enjoy it! Half dead with flu, standing on a verandah in the depths of winter, I needed a cold can of half beer, half soda water about as much as an Ethiopian refugee needs a year's supply of Limmits.

We finally got that part done then it was off next day to another glamorous location, Rydal, 30km west of Goulburn.

I thought Windsor was cold. You should see this joint in the middle of August. It's like the Sino-Soviet border.

It was still overcast and we were all huddled around in two blankets trying to stay alive.

I was sneezing worse than ever and coughing up pieces of lungs while the director ran around burning hubcaps full of kerosene under the camera lens to give it a heat-haze effect. Then every time the sun came out the wardrobe lady whipped the blankets off us, sprayed us with water to make us look like we were sweating and we'd all get in front of the camera and tell each other how hot it was.

Then the locals came down with their banjos and shotguns to check us out.

I'll say one thing about Rydal: they keep sex off the streets and in the family down there. There were kids there with webbed fingers and toes the creature from the black lagoon would have envied. Girls with three eyes; all different colours. Blokes in funny-looking hats with ears big enough to swat flies with.

I went over to their tiny, one-man pub for a double brandy and even the beer had two heads.

But the locals decided against shooting or burning any of us so we got the thing shot and got out of town.

Which, for me, meant dodging giant coal trucks back to Terrigal on the Central Coast in a rusted-out Datsun 1600 that let the freezing cold wind in and the rain, which began pissing down five minutes past Goulburn.

I got home and spent the next two weeks in bed with what was more like bronchial pneumonia than flu. After paying for my petrol, doctor's bills, agent's fees plus tax, I made SFA.

Why am I telling you all this? Just for all the mugs out there who think TV commercials are all glitz and glamour.

As far as I'm concerned, Resch's is the worst beer on the market. It tastes like tomcat's piss and you wouldn't give it to a Nazi war criminal during Yom Kippur.

BORE it up 'em, BRUCE

I'm a dead-set goose. I had my one giant chance with this column to make a big man of myself and I blew it.

When I should have bagged Bruce Ruxton and called him a racist and gone on and on, like a mug I turned around and said I didn't mind him.

If I'd rubbished Ruxton 15 per cent of Australia would have been my oyster. The ABC would have loved me, trendy radio stations would have interviewed me on prime time, Jane Singleton would have taken me to her breast, along with all the rest of the bleeding hearts in the media.

I reckon even Trish Goddard would have forgiven me for saying she had a backside like the end of a Ford Louisville.

But I have to open my big mouth and say he's all right.

And he is to a certain extent. You know what Ruxton's trouble is, apart from being a white Australian with an Anglo-Saxon name? He speaks out on Asian migration, bags certain black Africans like Bishop Desmond Tutu and he told a few truths about the Japanese.

You see it's very trendy and self-righteous to dump on blokes like Bruce Ruxton and Geoff Blainey no matter what they say, even if it makes a certain amount of sense. Rubbish them and you really make it among the holier-than-thou shining knights in the media and their hangers-on. In other words you're not a … yes, you know the dreaded word, a racist.

So let's have a look at what bouncing Bruce baby said that has made him such a dropkick in the eyes of, according to the polls, 15 per cent of Australians.

First he said he wasn't opposed to Asian immigration. He just didn't want to see Australia turned into another Hong Kong, that's all. Which I think is fair enough.

There are about four billion Asians out there who would love to live in Australia. We could let 50 million in and it wouldn't even be a drop in the bucket.

However, to discriminate against these people would not only be bigoted, it would be plain stupid. If we did, we wouldn't have any Jenny Kees or Dr Victor Changs here. And believe me, this country needs all the people of that calibre it can get.

But Australia doesn't have to be a dumping ground for rich Asians of dubious means and so-called refugees. I'm sure the abovementioned people must cringe when they read about Chinese and Singaporean syndicates running heroin into the country. And gangs of Vietnamese youths shooting each other and bursting into houses, stealing the contents and beating old ladies to death. Game bastards, aren't they? And they certainly show their appreciation for us letting them out here.

But don't try to deport the little turds. The bleeding hearts will let them hire a QC at the taxpayers' expense and he'd beat you hands down.

Then Ruxton said what a lot of bastards the Japanese were during the war and they're not much better now, the way they're buying out Australia thanks to mugs like Skase and Bond.

He went into bat for all the old diggers when they opposed the idea of building a memorial to the Japanese sailors who died entering Sydney Harbour in their midget submarines during WWII.

I reckon it's okay to build a memorial to them. As soon as the Jews build a memorial to all the Nazi SS troopers who died putting down the uprising in the Warsaw ghetto. And when the Russians build one to all the German soldiers who died during the siege of Stalingrad.

Incidentally, if those Japanese sailors had reached their objective and blown up the USS *Chicago* with all its explosives on board, we wouldn't have a harbour to build a memorial on.

The other thing that Bruce Ruxton said that caused him to be pilloried by the do-gooders and for some hero to beat up 60-year-old Ruth Ruxton, was that half of those black Africans are a bunch of whingers and he called old Bishop Tutu a witchdoctor.

He's pretty right here again too. Those black African nations put on all the dramas about the place over apartheid to get sympathy and millions of dollars in aid to prop up what are nothing more than corrupt dictatorships. And governments like ours can't kiss their backsides quick enough to seek appeasement in the eyes of the world.

From what I can see, apartheid is a pretty loathsome idea but I'm convinced the majority of these black Africans are dreading the day it ends.

They'll have nothing to whinge about. Same with their grandstanding supporters out here.

I wonder what the next cause they'll embrace will be? I'll bet it isn't the Aboriginal elders dying out on the missions and the riverbeds.

As for calling Tutu a witchdoctor, I reckon that's hilarious. I could just picture this shyster with a bone through his nose covered in blood and chicken feathers.

This grandstanding old showpony has been hamming it up in front of the crowds worse than Dame Edna. All he needs when he comes out in front of the TV cameras rolling his eyes is a bunch of gladioli.

A witchdoctor is a reasonable comparison. I reckon he's more like a black Ian Paisley. Full of religion but not a drop of Christianity.

Anyway, good on you Bruce, baby. Bore it up 'em! Kick a few backsides and tread on a few toes. And if you need a hand, give me a yell and you can borrow my 10-hole Doc Martens.

DUCK! It's the SILLY SEASON again

The duck shooting season is an annual event that all Australians can be proud of.

It's the time when about 20,000 drunken morons get full of piss, put on their cammies, grab a shotgun, then go out into the countryside to find a lake and blast everything that flies out of the sky.

Kookaburras, Willie wagtails, swans, herons, even tortoises. You name it, these loaded imbeciles will shoot it.

And it's supposed to be a sport. This isn't a sport. It's nothing more than a sadistic bloody slaughter by a crowd of twits who can't or haven't the brains to find a better way to get their rocks off.

Crazy, isn't it? And, instead of arresting a mob of drunks running around with shotguns, the cops arrest those trying to stop the suffering of poor defenceless animals. People with a bit more in their veins than booze.

If you don't believe me, come down to Martin Place in Sydney during the duck shooting season when the people from The Fund For Animals and Animal Liberation carry around the evidence of what a mob of drunken idiots consider is a weekend of fun — dead ibises, parrots, magpies, swans, tortoises — even if it doesn't fly, those heroes will still shoot it.

Then they'll take the mutilated animals up to State Parliament and dump them out the front.

There'll be more cops out the front ready to arrest any crying children or people with a bit of intelligence that try to come near the MPs. They're as gutless as the clowns with the shotguns.

I'm not against the genuine sports shooter — the person who knows his/her rifle and goes out into the bush and using some skill, hunts for feral animals. These people do show a bit of professionalism and do the bush a favour.

I used to hunt rabbits for a feed when I lived in the bush. But what chance has a poor little bird got against a shotgun? None. You can't bloody miss. And these dopes like to think they're macho men. They're enough to make you spew.

What about all the lakes they pollute with their shotgun pellets? There is literally tons of lead out there seeping into the water-table.

The government's talking (whispering) about bringing in tighter gun control. This is a good enough reason to ban the sale of shotguns. And I don't think I'd get any argument there from the police.

One thing I've noticed, when TV crews go down to the lakes the weekend Rambos run for cover. They're not too keen to be shown standing next to all the unfortunate bloody animals they've killed.

So I'll hand out an invitation to all the heroes of the hunt. When the duck season starts come down to Martin Place and Parliament House. Wear your cammies and your bandoliers and bring your shotguns. And get a few photos and go on TV standing next to all those dead swans, pelicans, ibises and tortoises.

And you can tell Australia the thrill and joy of blasting a swan or a tortoise with a shotgun. Or watching a poor, wretched bird flop around in a lake, dying in agony. It must be a great feeling. Almost as good as the pull they have afterwards, I imagine.

But normal thinking people and those in The Fund For Animals and Animal Liberation can take some heart. Even though it's not much there is some good that comes out of the duck season.

Occasionally, some of these drunken idiots shoot each other.

ME NUDE! You must be STARK raving MAD

I was sitting at home not doing a great deal when the phone rang.

It was the editor of *People*, Peter Olszewski. He had an assignment for me. They were opening a $6 million resort at Port Stephens — Bardots. It was near my place. Why don't I go and cover it?

Why not indeed? Free food and drink. Swanky resort, glamour scene. Just the sort of thing a writer of my calibre deserves. And what a good bloke Peter was to send me there.

Only one minor problem — I didn't have a car. I'd just smashed mine in the last deluge.

So I rang my mate Steve, one of the leading chefs on NSW's Central Coast. I owed him a favour. Would he like to be my assistant for the day? All he had to do was carry an Instamatic and make out he's with *People*. Free food and piss. I'll pay for the petrol. The opening of an ultra-swish resort.

Steve was round my place at nine the next morning with the hatchback all schmicked up and keener than a greyhound that had just been given a kill.

That @#*%*! Olszewski. Bardots was a resort all right. And an upmarket, ultra-swish one. For bloody nudists!

I know what was on the bastard's mind. Send me to cover it and I've got to get around with no gear on. Me in all my glory — 90kg of dynamite with a 1cm fuse.

We arrived at another resort where the function was being held and there were all these ads for nudism: posters, videos, films and such.

Steve reckoned he wasn't getting his clobber off. To me it was part of the job. I could stand the sniggers if they could stand the smell. Anyway, seeing I was there in the midst of a lot of nice and, so far, well-dressed people, I thought I'd better earn my keep and take down a few notes.

The first person I interviewed was Tracy, a tall blonde model. And what have you been up to lately, Tracy?

'I did a streak at the Newcastle trots,' cooed Tracy, 'and it was on SKY channel.'

Terrific, Tracy. You got arrested and three million drunks and punters across Australia have seen your lamington.

What else? Tracy ran something called Fantasy Girls and she did mud wrestling. She also wrestled in baked beans, jelly and spaghetti full of baby oil and lumps of fluorescent paint.

The good-looking bloke with her scratching his arse all the time was another model, Ray.

Fleas bad, Ray?

No. Ray was a male stripper with the Big Boys. About 50 drunken housewives had tried to pack rape him in the dressing room of a Newcastle club and both cheeks of his bum were covered in love bites.

I took some more notes then we all went inside where Professor Magnus Clarke from *University Challenge* was giving an address because he's a nudist himself.

Magnus looks like TV presenter Iain Finlay wearing one of Brian Bury's bow ties. His address was witty and interesting at first — then it just seemed to go on and on forever like episodes of M*A*S*H.

He had us at first, till he had to let us all know he had a PhD. Nudism is not an ideology. It's an activity. The human body has a long history. Nudism was not forced upon people through penury. Evil be to him who evil thinks.

They finally got the professor off and Tracy and Ray got their gear off and jumped in the pool for a photo session.

About the same time Steve and I found a friendly barman with access to an unlimited supply of imported beer.

We ripped into this and scarcely had time to get roaring drunk when they started wheeling out all this grouse food. Teriyaki beef, Atlantic salmon, beautiful crisp salads and fruits the names of which I couldn't even pronounce. The kind of food they're going to be dishing up at Bardots.

I asked Steve what he thought and he gave it a huge thumbs up. And Steve ought to know — he's a chef. We were tearing into all this beautiful food and cold beer when we were told a cruise on Port Stephens had been arranged — the boat was leaving in 40 minutes.

Steve and I pigged out a bit more, got a neat T-shirt each and headed for the marina.

Outside we were asked directions by two strange looking young women with Sydney Stadium haircuts, Jack Nicholson sunnies, severe clothes and Doc Martens with bits of metal on them.

Hello, Steve and I thought. It's The Women Against Rape In Nudist Colonies. But it turned out they'd been sent along by the ABC. Same bloody thing.

The boat was a beaut. It was like a small Manly ferry with heaps of room and cruised through the swells like a '38 Bentley.

The best part was the skipper Peter Dawson and his wife Penny. As we chugged gently along, as well as pointing out the sights, he bombarded us with gags and one-liners that seemed to be directed at his wife. But we all roared with laughter — mainly because they kept bringing out all this beautiful Hunter Valley champagne and cheeses and things.

We were on the other side of the bay sipping champers when Steve said he could smell garlic.

Penny was heating this huge pot of garlic prawns that had just been caught that morning. She served them with two monstrous loaves of oven-fresh bread.

You reckon the hordes didn't give these unbelievable garlic prawns a serve?

I was going to ask Steve what he thought of them but the last I saw of him he had Penny by the throat near the stern trying to force the recipe out of her.

We cruised on, drinking more champagne, taking in the sights and, before we knew it, we were back at the marina. We thanked Jim and Vicki Punch, the owners of Bardots, and everyone else for a top day then Steely Danned it back to Terrigal.

It was definitely one up for yours truly. Olszewski thought he'd got me. But no, I didn't have to take my gear off. All I had to do was eat grouse food, drink cold beer and meet nice people.

REAL MEN save WHALES

I give a certain amount from the royalties on my books to Greenpeace — and I am a noted tightwad.

People query why I do this. Is it to big-note myself or just to help sell books?

They also wonder why a person who puts so much blood and guts and violence in his books could support an organisation that's into pansy things like saving baby dolphins, little animals and trees.

It's not very good for the macho man image.

Well, frankly Scarlett, I don't give a stuff.

I reckon Greenpeace is the most selfless, dedicated organisation in the world and probably the best thing this planet's got going for it at the moment. And that's not taking anything away from the Australian Conservation Foundation, the Wilderness Society and people like Phillip Toyne and Peter Garrett.

The feats Greenpeace pulls off and the glare of the spotlight it turns on the bastards that want to destroy what's left of our planet is phenomenal.

I truly admire these brave people, yet you know what thanks and support they get from governments the world over?

Zilch.

The first people the cops arrest are the ones from Greenpeace.

You never see the arrest of a captain or crew of some ship dumping poison in the North Sea or off Tasmania.

You'll never see the manager of a company like ICI put in gaol or fined for pumping millions of litres of industrial waste into the ocean.

No way. But as soon as Greenpeace arrives on the scene the cops are there in droves. And they reckon there's a police shortage!

Look at some of the things Greenpeace does and figure it out for yourself why I give what support I can.

Its campaigners get out in rubber dinghies, in the middle of nowhere, in appalling weather conditions and dangerous seas to get between a Japanese harpoon gun and a whale swimming with her calf.

The Japs have stuffed our prawn and tuna industry; now they're effectively turning the ocean into a stagnant pond with their driftnets.

Who gets out there and tries to free the thousands of birds, seals, dolphins and other animals from drowning and bring the world's attention to this environmental atrocity?

It was Greenpeace which stopped those moronic Canadians from clubbing baby harp seals to death by again showing the world what was going on — they got out on the ice-floes to spray the pups with green dye and risked getting drowned and clubbed themselves.

They won the battle and, again, what thanks did they get?

Again they were arrested; this time by the Canadian cops.

What about the bloke who swam 10km underwater to free so many thousand dolphins the kindly Japanese fishermen had penned up ready to slaughter with harpoons and pikes for eating their fish?

THEIR bloody fish?

And what thanks did this hero get?

Again the cops arrested him, the Japs this time, and he got five years' gaol.

They should have given him a knighthood.

Oddly enough, if he'd been a member of the Queensland National Party and bulldozed a rainforest then taken about half a million dollars in bribes he'd have got one — they might even have made him Premier.

And while on the subject of the Japanese ... If ever there was a nation of bastards when it comes to the environment it would have to be these sub-humans.

They're ruining the forests and the oceans and they have the bloody hide to come out here taking photos of the dolphins at Monkey Mia and the whales at Hervey Bay. And we're all expected to kiss their arses because they buy our coal and wool.

A few old ex-POWs reckon they should get *Enola Gay* out of mothballs and go in and give them another serve.

But I especially like the macho men in the media and government who try to look tough by bagging Greenpeace: Alan Jones, John Laws, that troglodyte WA senator Peter Walsh, the politician Ian Causley and his pals in the National Party.

Though I can understand Lawsie talking tough on the environment; he does have his Valvoline-in-the-jeep, blue-denim, Jim Beam image to keep up.

Maybe Lawsie might like to get out in a rubber dinghy dodging harpoons and toxic waste.

It might not be as good for the image but it would have to be as macho as driving a jeep.

Then again, driving a jeep is a bit of a feat and you could fall out and ruin a perfectly good hair-transplant.

And I can dig members of the National Party hating Greenpeace and calling all environmentalists long-haired gits.

If it wasn't for these long-haired freaks and their ilk a bit more of our coastline would be gone and the beaut pulp mill would be destroying the forests and polluting the ocean and rivers around Grafton.

Though I can't quite see how they manage to call Peter Garrett a long-haired git.

The man has a degree — and he's as bald as a badger.

So I support Greenpeace, I always will and I hope some day to be able to do more than the little I do now.

I love nature and I prefer these people and wildlife to some of the poor excuses there are for human beings running around the world today — especially some of those politicians and media identities.

Who's JACK of ROBBO?

I don't know what the average punter gets to watch on late-night TV in other states, but around Sydney there's nothing much to get enthused over. Especially in the 10.30–11.30 spot.

The various channels appear to have run completely out of imagination during this time.

For a while we used to have an hour of smut and innuendo with Graham Kennedy on Channel Nine, but the King did us a favour by abdicating.

We had Steve Vizard on Channel Seven; he thought he was David Letterman and looked like Don Lane with Phar Lap's teeth.

Re-runs of *Dallas* on Channel 10. Seemingly endless politics and news on the ABC. And either the Iranian public stoning finals or the Saudi Arabian beheading tournament on SBS.

It's a pretty skinny go, I can tell you.

Then, amidst a veritable avalanche of hype and publicity, we got the return of a thing called Clive Robertson, who filled the hole Kennedy left at Nine.

Has anybody out there in the real world of workers and battlers ever seen or heard Clive Robertson?

It's something else, believe me.

Clive kicked off in radio's sheltered workshop, 2BL in Sydney.

Here he is supposed to have built-up a cult following amongst butterfly collectors, tea-leaf readers and various pixies and goblins found in the gardens on Sydney's lower north shore, with his alleged droll sense of humour.

Financial genius and entrepreneurial hero Christopher Skase took over Channel Seven and gave Clive the 10.30–11.30 spot reading the news and trying to be titillatingly amusing at the same time.

Clive sat there wearing the same Gowings suit and the same boring regimental-striped tie, peering through his specs, shuffling papers around and grunting out these droll comments like bowel movements.

I used to watch this with a sense of déjà vu.

Then it dawned on me.

Clive always reminded me of a government doctor in a VD clinic.

I got the jack years ago and had to go to the VD clinic near Circular Quay in Sydney. The old blue light. The House That Jack Built.

Clive Robertson looks exactly like a pox doctor.

Same boring tie, same chatty suit, same supercilious smile and the same smug look when they say: 'You've got gonorrhoea'.

Then shove a needle the size of a bike-pump in your arse and smirk as you try to negotiate the stairs, barely able to walk.

It's always amazed me how Clive Robertson achieved this star status.

There are not enough Bs in boring to describe the big mummy's boy.

He's fat and bald, got more chins than a Hong Kong phone book and blinks through those glasses like an owl with a strangulated hernia.

He doesn't run, doesn't swim, doesn't go to the beach and thinks that anyone who tries to keep fit is an idiot.

He hates sport and barbecues, and he goes on like a misogynist.

He detests rock'n'roll music and refuses to have football or boxing on the news.

He's never been drunk, never copped a whack on the chin, never had his dabs taken and it's extremely doubtful if he'd have even half a good root in him.

Clive's idea of an exciting evening is crocheting tea-cosies while listening to Tchaikovsky's violin concerto in D major, op 35.

And this is a typical Australian male allowed to influence public opinion TV.

Somebody should kick him right up his fat arse and drag him back into the real world.

I hear there are a few camera crews around who would gladly do it too.

Clive spat the dummy at Seven around the same time as Skase hit the skids, and spent about six months picking his toes and sucking his thumb till 2GB in Sydney offered him a gig.

He and another equally-opinionated bore, Mike Jeffreys, were primed up in yet another blaze of hype and publicity to take on the arch-villain of Sydney radio: John Laws.

The mongrel. They were going to whip John Laws' arse so bad.

'Hello, Jeffreys and Robertson,' they'd smirk over the phone to any mug silly enough to ring them up.

It sounded like the name of a hardware store in Coonabarabran.

And away they'd go, each trying to out do the other's droll comment, dry sense of humour or acerbic witticism.

And what a pair of cutie-pies.

Unfortunately, Jeffreys and Robertson were just a bit too clever for this world.

They should have greased their arses and slipped into the next.

They went over like a pregnant woman pole-vaulting. In less than 12 months they were rating alongside the Marcel Marceau hour on 2MBS-FM.

Eventually their drollness and dryness caught up with them and they drolled right down the steps of 2GB and blew away in the breeze.

And you wonder why. On three separate occasions I did a bit of dial switching between the mongrel and Snugglepot and Cuddlepie just to see what was going on.

On the first occasion, Mike and Clive were talking about sandwich fillings; John Laws was interviewing the treasurer, Paul Keating.

The second time they were discussing recipes for scones (I'm fair dinkum); the mongrel was interviewing the boss of Ansett at the height of the pilots' dispute.

The third time Mike Jeffreys and Clive Robertson were comparing the designs on their underpants. John Laws was interviewing the PM.

Which I think just about sums up Clive Robertson.

Come back Don Lane. All is forgiven.

Keystone KOPS meet POLICE Academy 6

I haven't been having a great deal of luck in the acting and TV commercial rort lately.

The castings have been there and so have about a thousand other blokes a lot less fat, bald and ugly than me.

And when I do crack one I either wreck my car, get beaten to a pulp or end up in bed with pneumonia.

However, the people with the big cigars — my agents — tipped me into one the other week that they said would be a snack.

No lines to learn, no fight scenes, all I had to do was stand in a bar and act the laconic Australian shearer in an ABC telemovie *Gunshearer*.

The call sheet arrived shortly after and sure enough there was no dialogue. All I had to do was lob up to the Native Rose Hotel in inner-Sydney's Chippendale at 10 p.m., one quick scene.

Beauty. I had a few things to take care of in town, I could see a movie, stay the night at a mate's place, I'd be finished by midnight tops — even allowing for the ABC — get everything finished in the morning and be home before I knew it. Suits me to the ground.

Naturally it was pissing rain when I left Terrigal and crawled all the way to Sydney in the traffic, but managed to get a couple of things done and I did get to see a movie.

When I walk out of the movie it's pissing rain worse than ever.

I got to the pub all right and the only sign of activity was the lighting man coughing and spluttering into the gutter. He told me the humidity played up with his asthma.

I went inside and met the bright-eyed and bushy-tailed director, the other shearers and the two blokes playing the detectives. I then found out I had some waffle and dialogue after all.

And as they were a bit tight on scripts they asked if we could ad-lib as much as possible. My little scene had me and another shearer playing pool and acting evasive as the two cops question us about the murder of another shearer.

Which sort of suited me. I've been acting evasive with the wallopers all my life. The first lesson they taught us at Bondi Beach Public School was, never make a statement.

So I slipped into my R.M. Williams and after a bit of stuffing around ABC-style it was roll film, and away we went.

After a bit I started to get the hang of it. I grunted my lines out the side of my mouth and, like I predicted, it was all done by midnight.

I was about to leg it when the bright-eyed and bushy-tailed director said to stick around.

He wanted me for the fight scene.

Fight scene? It didn't say anything in my call sheet about a bloody fight scene. But I was stuck there and they still had to shoot another scene with a uniformed cop questioning the barmaid. It was 2.30 a.m. and my eyes were hanging out of my head when they finished it. The action is supposed to take place in a dry and deserted bush town — the ABC, in its wisdom, chose an inner-city hotel while it was pissing rain, with cars and trucks roaring past the door every five seconds.

Finally, between breaks in the traffic, they got it shot. Then it was on to the fight scene where the drunken shearer starts arguing over a game of pool and the publican throws him out.

It was getting late and by now I was in no mood for any ad-libbing. I thought the best thing for me to do was play the full-on laconic Outback Aussie. So I propped my arse on a stool, held my pool cue and watched as the director and the other actors floundered around the pool table.

By 3 a.m. I was laconic-ed to the point of numbness and the fight scene wasn't getting anywhere.

I had to put my head in or we'd be here till dawn. So I told the director about some of the fights I'd seen in pubs over pool tables where the antagonists did swear and say nasty things to each other, grapple and rend each other's clothing and throw pool cues and other items around in a manner most violent.

It soon livened up. There was about 45 minutes of 'Piss off arsehole!', 'Get stuffed' and 'Why don't ya stick your pub up your arse?', push, shove, grapple, fling the pool cue. After the publican speared the shearer out the door amidst plenty of noise it was finally over — and I was released.

I bolted straight for my car. I was just about to open the door when … 'wow-wow-wow-wow-wow'. Blue lights flashing, sirens wailing as they screeched to a stop outside the pub. Cops. Real ones. Mean and lots of them.

It seems the neighbours rang the police and said there was a monstrous fight going on at the Native Rose and they were wrecking the joint.

Out they jumped. Hats off, batons at the ready, blood in their eyes. And the first bloke they decided to smash up was the poor bloody lighting bloke having another asthma attack.

They were just about to give him the NSW Police Force's idea of a fair-go when I yelled to cool it. It was only a movie. And a dud one at that.

I took a couple of photos, which didn't go down too well with the cops so I took off. So much for *Gunshearer* on the ABC. It was more like the *Keystone Kops meet Police Academy 6*. Though at 4 a.m., you'll forgive me if I didn't quite see the funny side of it.

Of BIG WETS and BIGGER HEARTS

My dear old dad, God rest his soul, was a great one for home-spun sayings.

One of his favourites was: 'I used to complain that I had no shoes, till I met a man who had no feet.'

A few weeks ago we copped a heap of rain in Sydney and up here on the Central Coast.

There was some minor flooding; a number of homes were damaged.

My garage got half-full of water, the guttering around the house choked up with leaves and rotted through in parts, and there was mould all over the walls and in my wardrobe.

I whinged, I whined, moaned and groaned and carried on like a good sort because I had to scrub out the garage and get up on the roof and clean out the gutters.

Fair dinkum, the hardships and suffering the rain caused me was almost too much to bear. I think back on it now — and the way I carried on — and I wish a great big boot, about a size 20, would come out of the sky and kick me fair up the arse — and hard.

For the past week or so I've been watching TV and reading the papers and I've seen what the people of Nyngan and Charleville have just gone through. In fact, in that whole stretch from Dubbo to Longreach.

These people haven't just had a few inches of water in their garage or a clogged-up gutter.

These poor bastards have lost practically everything. Their homes, possessions, farms, livestock. Their towns. Some have even lost their lives.

You know, we in the cities and towns and roundabouts take things pretty much for granted.

You want a dozen eggs or a bit of bacon? Just stroll or drive down to the shop and get it. Milk, loaf of bread, some tomatoes? The same.

Coles and Woolies don't make food in their parking lots. It comes from a lot of sweat out in the bush.

That litre of milk. Some dairy farmer's got up at dawn and slogged through mud and manure to get you that.

Those tomatoes. Some farmer's probably busted his arse to grow those. He's had to take a punt on the weather, crop failure, locusts and God knows what else to try to make ends meet. Then at the end, hope to Christ the bank doesn't foreclose on the loan they've given him at exorbitant rates and kick him off his land.

And now these people and others that depend on them are devastated. They've done the lot.

Imagine the position they're in. Their homes, their incomes, their properties — gone. What's left is ruined. Insurance won't cover it. When does it ever?

The most they expect is about $5000 from the government.

Not much to restart your life with, is it? It's not just the homes that are gone. Farmers, along with losing all their stock, have had to watch all their topsoil being washed away. What do they grow those tomatoes in now? Bedrock?

Was anybody not moved by those scenes on TV?

Farmers having to walk around paddocks of mud shooting all their stock. Sheep and cattle stuck in mud just waiting to die a cruel, rain-sodden death.

The effort those people in Nyngan put in to try to save their town, packing almost half-a-million sandbags. Women in their 60s working non-stop from seven in the morning till seven at night.

Blokes like Ken Cobcroft, a shearer: 'I've had three hours sleep in three days,' he said. 'Then the water backed up two metres on the railway line and flooded the other side of town anyway.'

Four days and four nights these people worked their guts out only to have the flood beat them in the end.

Sure there were some tears as they were being evacuated, but I think one woman summed up their feelings and their bush stoicism. As she got on the helicopter after losing everything she had, and with nothing but the clothes she was wearing, she looked at the TV camera, smiled and said: 'Oh well. That's bush life.'

I don't know what it is they've got out in Nyngan but I wish you could bottle it.

So now it looks like the rest of us are being asked to put our hands in our kicks and give a bit of help.

Like Wayne Goss, the Premier of Queensland, said: 'The government just can't come up with an open cheque.'

And that's fair enough. It's up to the rest of us. And about bloody time too.

We, and the government, give away millions of dollars overseas to trendy causes and charities.

Let's help our fellow Australians for a change. I reckon charity begins at home.

You *People* readers please yourself where you send your donations.

You'll see the government ads in the newspapers and hear them on your local radio station. I gave mine to my building society.

I just couldn't picture myself leaving a donation with the bank.

All banks seem to specialise in is crippling farmers with interest rates then kick them off their farms.

But, whatever you do, don't bother sending these people any ticker.

They've still got plenty of that.

Oh, by the way. A big cheerio to all the city readers.

I'm sure they must all be very proud of a certain Sydney gent who was arrested for allegedly looting, malicious damage, driving while disqualified and stealing a 4WD belonging to Ray Travern of Nyngan while Ray was helping to build a levee bank.

LOVE thy neighbour

It's not easy to write about death. Writing about life is hard enough.

I think it was Joseph Stalin who said: 'A single death is a tragedy. A million deaths is a statistic.'

But there was a death in our street not so long ago. The doctor across the road's wife died — she was about 80.

Not that I ever met the doc or his wife. In the eight years I've been here I never said a word to either of them.

The only time I ever got to see the good doctor was when he drove into town at a steady, concerned citizen's pace of 25km/h and I would join a kilometre-long convoy of cursing, screaming drivers trying to get round the old dropkick.

In fact, I haven't had a great deal to do with my neighbours at all. I was their worst nightmare come true — an under-75 moving into the street.

From the day I bought my block of land I was treated like a cross between Charles Manson and a full-blown AIDS carrier.

I was a battling, out-of-work butcher trying to build a house with the money I got from a compo claim after stuffing my shoulder and almost breaking my back. But you would have thought it was Joseph Mengele who flew in from Paraguay and hung his shingle in the street. It started even before the builders had laid a brick.

I was sitting on my block of land one day, listening to the races on a little transistor radio, when Lucrezia Borgia swooped down and ordered me to take the radio to the other side of my land and 'TURN THE THING DOWN'.

(On the subject of death: you ought to see this pair living near me. If they were in the funeral business, people would stop dying.)

But I turned the radio down. And the next day I returned with a ghetto blaster and a couple of Rose Tattoo tapes. The first two bars of 'Bad Boy For Love' had Lucrezia foaming at the mouth and sent her poor dopey husband's pacemaker into warp–7. Lucrezia organised the para-military senior citizens and from then it was on. I had an old ute which I left on my land and they put a FOR SALE sign on it and dumped rubbish in it.

When the builders started work they complained to the council about the noise. They complained about the Porta-loo out the front. It stunk. Yet all the builders used it for was storing bags of cement out of the weather.

They complained about the builders listening to a radio while they worked. One old codger even capped his tap so the builders couldn't get a drink of water in the middle of summer.

They complained about the noise from me feeding parrots. They complained if there was nothing to complain about.

So I thought, well, why not put all their pacemakers into hyper-drive? I had a word with the builders.

One morning the concerned citizens awoke to find a sign on my land saying: 'Spanish And Colonial Homes. A Block Of Six Home Units To Be Erected On This Site.'

I kept away for a while then one weekend I went to the site with Lee, a barmaid I was going with at the time … a truly lovely girl I promised faithfully to marry if she'd help me move two tonnes of boulders, about the same amount of logs and clear all the lantana off my land. Then change the gearbox and diff in the old ute.

We were walking up from the bottom of my land and there they were. All the concerned citizens, formed into a baying vigilante mob laying in wait for me, hissing. All that was missing was a rope, an old feather mattress and a bucket of hot tar.

'Are you the owner of this block of land?' thundered the spokesperson for the concerned citizens.

'Yes. That's right,' I replied.

'What's this … this sign? A block of home units to be erected here.'

He could hardly get the words out as the mob pressed closer.

'That's right,' I said. 'I'm doing a bit of speculating. Making a few quick dollars.'

'You can't build units in this street. Don't you know about clause splimpty-seven? Bylaw eleventy-two A? The council won't allow it.'

'The council? Hah! They're as good as gold in there, mate.' Making the appropriate hand gesture, I continued: 'Just sling them enough and you can do anything you like.'

I had them in and I could have kept it up all day only silly bloody Lee started laughing. And I cracked up too. I had to confess that I'd put it there for a joke: 'Just to see if I could get any mugs in.'

Somehow, my neighbours failed to see the funny side of it and they never spoke to me again; they hated me and I ignored them — unless ratface and his missus sent the police around to my house for some reason or other.

After about four years I decided to mow the front lawn and the bloke across the road must have figured I'd turned into a solid citizen and informed me of the good doctor's wife passing away. So what did I do? Kind, caring, compassionate soul that I am, I put a card in his letter-box.

And people read this column and write in and call me a dickhead and a bastard. It was more than my neighbours did for me when my cat Achmet died.

Living with DERRYN the DUNNART

Being involved with Greenpeace can be rewarding; you know you're helping a good cause and you get to meet some of the nicest people imaginable.

It can also be a complete bummer because you're supposed to respect the environment no matter what and, above all, you're not allowed to kill anything.

I was watching TV the other night and a rat ran across my loungeroom.

Now I don't care if you're a greenie, a Buddhist monk or St Francis of Assisi. A rat is a rat whether it's baked, boiled or grilled on a stick in Ethiopia. And this particular rat had to go. So I lay in wait wondering what to do. Trap it, poison it, get a gun and blow the bastard away?

While I was figuring the best way to go about it the rat just went about its business, helping itself to the tucker then going back to wherever it was dossing as an uninvited guest in my house.

It certainly didn't seem worried by me.

Then one night it ambled across the lounge and propped under the TV looking at me. And I thought, Christ, it's got a funny nose for a rat and it didn't look at all like those horrible black things I used to see in Bondi, plus its ears seemed rounder.

So I checked it out on my poster from the National Parks and Wildlife Service.

And it wasn't a rat — it was a dunnart, a protected species in NSW and I couldn't harm it, let alone kill it.

So it was back to the drawing board.

By now the dunnart had twigged it was on to a pretty good thing and that I was a 24-carat mug. It began to treat me with utter disdain.

I'd be watching TV or something and it would come out, very casually, and head straight for the kitchen.

It kicked off just eating bananas and apples and so on, then soon developed a more exotic taste, gnawing its way through my Kiwi fruit and peaches.

It wouldn't eat the white bread I fed to the lorikeets, straight into the rye. And what thanks did I get?

The thing crapped everywhere. Hundreds and hundreds of little turds like big, black grape pips.

Not only that, it just came and went with complete impunity. I didn't expect the thing to get down on its hands and knees and thank me for being a good bloke.

But, after all, it is my bloody house so surely I command a modicum of respect. But no. Kiss my arse. Protected or not, the dunnart had to go.

But what could I do? Imagine if I shot it and Hinch found out? He'd have a field day. Shame, shame, shame. Drunken, lewd author and convicted drug offender posing as Greenpeace activist slaughters protected species in blood-drenched carnage of wanton wildlife destruction and butchery. Shame R.G. Barrett, shame.

Actually, by now this dunnart with its hairy, rat-like little face began to remind me of Derryn Hinch, which I reckon is a good enough excuse to kill anything.

Then one night I was in my office and Derryn the dunnart came in after a feed and ran into the inbuilt wardrobe.

I jumped up, slammed the doors and stacked books all along the bottom of the wardrobe so it couldn't get out.

Got the little bastard!

The next morning I tossed in half a Kiwi fruit (one of Derryn's favourites) with a few downers in it.

I figured that ought to at least knock the little bludger out then I could take it safely to a tranquil, bushland setting and release it to run wild with all its little furry friends once more.

Then I got involved in something or other and completely forgot about Derryn for three days.

Christ! I thought. I'd better get the bloody thing out before it starts to stink the place up.

I opened the wardrobe but no dunnart and no Kiwi fruit.

I don't now what the tranquillisers did to it, but it ate its way out.

It ate through my $40 hardback edition of Hackworth's *About Face,* Le Carré's *The Honourable Schoolboy,* Hughes' *The Fatal Shore*, two *Hustlers* and about half a dozen old *Phantom* comics.

Derryn the dunnart didn't have a bad taste in literature. And he left about another hundred turds behind.

And now he's back, terrorising me more than ever. And it looks like he's brought a sheila with him.

Why wouldn't he? Can you imagine the line he's laid on some dunnart out there? 'Hey baby. Why don't you shack up with me? I got a pretty neat pad just up from the beach. The music's good. The tube's okay. There's plenty to eat. And, if you play it cool, every now and again you can score some unreal dope.'

A week's a LONG TIME in UKI

I got an invite to the Uki May Ball. 'Where's Uki?' you're probably wondering.

It's an old one-pub timber town near Mt Warning on the NSW North Coast.

Uki definitely isn't the Las Vegas of NSW and the May Ball doesn't attract the Sunday paper socialites.

But I'd made quite a few friends up that way and the Uki dance featured in my last book so I thought, for the sake of a bit of time and petrol, I ought to go back and have a look.

Plus a young lady in Coffs Harbour who liked my books had been writing nice letters so I thought I'd call in and see her and some other people I knew on the way.

I got in touch and arranged to take her out to dinner.

If nothing else, I am a romantic. I headed off on Friday morning and had a motel room in Coffs in the afternoon.

The young lady in question wasn't a bad sort, but she'd just turned 18 and was barely five foot tall. I don't mind cradle-snatching to a certain extent but to me this was making the gravy just a little bit thick. I was old enough to be this girl's uncle.

But we still went out for dinner and drinks and had a bloody good time. Yes, I did invite her back to my sleazy motel room, where we had a few drinks and a laugh and that was about it. Honest.

I got to Uki the following day but I brought the rain with me and plenty of it.

It had rained all day Friday on the property and it was still coming down on Saturday. But it didn't dampen the locals' enthusiasm for the May Ball and it was well away, a-reelin' and a-rockin' when I got there on Saturday night.

It was a gangsters-and-molls theme. I didn't know and didn't have the appropriate gear, but seeing I was still out on bail I was eligible for a consolation prize.

The turn was a ripper, the band was unreal, there was heaps of good, wholesome food and all proceeds went to the Uki Primary School.

I supplied some books to give away as door prizes and then stayed discreetly drunk in the background and popped off a few photos.

Some sheila with the biggest boobs I've ever seen came up and asked me to autograph a book for her.

I tried to be witty and scintillating but all I could put in the front of the book was: 'Jan. You've got the biggest tits I've ever seen.'

Then I showed these country hillbillies and young whippersnappers how to dance.

The Big River Boogie Band was belting it out raunchy enough to make your face turn blue.

Real funky, bluesy rock'n'roll. Music for dancing, not posing.

The thing I noticed at the dance again was all the kids running around. Not like those horrible dropkicks you see racing around shopping centres on skateboards smoking cigarettes. But good kids running around making heaps of noise and enjoying themselves.

You'd also think at a rock'n'roll turn there'd be broken glass and stinks everywhere, but it wasn't like that at all.

There was even a gang of bikers there but, compared to other bikers I've seen, I don't think any of this mob would have up-ended a Sao biscuit.

As for drugs — about two skinny joints went past my nose all night. I don't know how the politicians and the cops with their helicopters keep coming up with the multi-million-dollar drug raids. The average punter at the ball didn't look like he or she would have a pot to piss in.

Still, I suppose the government's got to look like it's earning its keep. And while the cops are arresting a few hippies they're not arresting each other.

In my last book, Les Norton gets a young spunk at the dance and ends up in a bubble bath with her back on the farm. All I looked like getting was blind drunk — and a 40-year-old with five kids. It was time for this grasshopper to leave.

I thanked them for the invite, wished everyone well and headed back to the farm in the pouring bloody rain.

I had intended hanging round the farm another day or so getting some photos and taking it easy, but when I got up on Sunday morning 'the crik had done rizz'. And that meant I had about half an hour to get my gear together or I'd be there for a week.

I packed in about 20 minutes, thanked my host and got going while the getting was good.

Uki's a nice little place, the people are good and I had a great weekend. But a week? That is making the gravy just a little bit too thick.

The BANKS: Bloody-minded BLOOD SUCKERS

One of my favourite one-liners goes: It was that cold this morning I saw the bank manager with his hands in his own pockets.

Which about sums up the banks very concisely.

There's hardly a day goes by when some bank heavy isn't threatening to do this or not do that.

Or they've pulled the rug from under some poor farmer and then sent the sheriff in to kick him off his land.

Or some poor punter's had to sell his house because the bank's put the interest rates up again.

Personally, I can't for the life of me see how sending businesses to the wall and squeezing ordinary working people into poverty with absolutely absurd interest rates is good for the economy.

Then, if they lend you $30,000 you pay back $75,000 and they go on as if they're doing you a big favour.

Their whole attitude in general amazes me.

I was lucky in that I didn't have to borrow a great deal to build my house and I got in on a supposedly fixed rate of interest — which the bank still managed to bump up an extra 1.5 per cent on the most abstruse technicality I have ever come across.

But I copped it sweet and did my best to keep the payments up.

I even went to gaol for my bank.

When I first moved in and was sent to the cleaners by the local builders, the local wallopers came banging on the door with a heap of parking summonses.

I had enough money to either pay the fines and stay free, or make a payment on the house and go in the pokey for a few days.

I chose the holiday at Gosford police cells resort sleeping on a wrestling mat with a blanket full of lice and my head next to a stainless-steel toilet bowl.

I did this to keep my bank manager happy.

These days it's hard to keep up the payments on your house.

Try making a living as a writer in Oz and you'll understand why.

But if you do get a bit behind?

It's not as though you're going anywhere. You can't pick up your house and land and put it on your back and piss off.

And what's a few lousy months between friends?

I've been with my bank for about 20 years. But they send letters and more letters.

And you get dragged in to see the bank manager which always reminds me of being paraded in front of the headmaster at school for a lecture and six of the best and don't be a naughty boy in future.

Then they send some bloke around, a bank agent, to spy on you and annoy you.

When I first saw the bank agent I thought he was collecting for the Smith Family.

His car was as daggy as mine. He had on a pair of pants with such a shiny backside that if he fell over he'd get seven years bad luck.

I told him to piss off.

In fact, I was that pissed off with the bank in general after 20 years, I thought I'd write them a letter — the one reprinted at the end of this story.

You must remember this was during a building boom on the Central Coast and I was feeling a bit cocky at the time.

About a month after I sent the letter Talking Books folded, I fell out with the film company and the property boom went bust.

Then I got a card in my letter-box saying there was a registered letter waiting for me at the post office.

I had a pretty good idea who it was from and I left it as long as I could.

Sure enough it was from my happy, friendly bank manager saying they wanted THE LOT in three weeks or they'd foreclose. Bastards. I may have had my one small moment but they had the last laugh.

I was once again forced to grovel.

And after grovelling and prostrating myself at my smiling, rotten bank manager's feet I was told, and I quote, 'I can put a lid on it for the time being'.

Worse. Not only was I made to grovel, I was forced to scrub pots in the stinkiest, hottest, smelliest kitchens on the Central Coast where no-one else would work.

This after my loyalty to the bank for 20 years. Bastards.

But I've got a feeling I'm going to kick on somehow and finish my mortgage in one go. Then revenge shall be mine.

I wonder what they give in the state of NSW for defecating on a bank manager's desk?

See if he can put a lid on that for the time being.

★ ★ ★ ★ ★

Dear Mr . . . .

Firstly, thank you for your kind, warm-hearted letters. It's always nice to know that your bank is still altruistic and you personally have my wellbeing and financial situation at heart. I appreciate it sincerely.

Now, as to my immediate financial situation. Well, I've got some good news and some bad news.

The bad news is I'm stone motherless broke and back on the dole. In fact I'm going that bad at the moment I was thinking of snipping you for a few bucks. Also my accountant has disappeared with all my receipts and this year's taxation return.

The good news is, my latest book made it to the best-selling list: 15,000 sold since November. And even though publishers in this country are almost on a par with banks for being miserable, parsimonious rapacious skinflints, I will still get a reasonable royalties cheque the first week in April.

I have also got rid of a shonky film producer who has been holding me up and I am about to sign up with PML Productions to make a movie out of my first book. The Recorded Book Company wants me to put my books down on cassette for the cretins in this country who are too lazy to read so some more money will be coming in there.

There could even be an earn for you.

I sold a story to a glossy magazine called *So You Want To Be An Awther*.

It comes out in June I think.

In it I have rubbished the Australian literary scene and the publishers and I referred to my bank manager as Snidely Von Bloodstone so you could have a chance to sue. That is if you can get through my lawyer who I referred to as Carnivore T. Funnelweb.

Apart from that nothing much else except that they sold the house three doors down from me for $280,000 about six weeks ago. Which is really disgusting when you think of the young couples trying to buy homes these days. And the houses in this street will probably go up again when they finish that Peppers On The Sea.

So in conclusion if your bank can struggle on until the first or second week in April I will catch up with whatever money I owe and this will save you the trouble of having to send the sheriff and a mob of thugs round to boot me out of my joint.

Yours faithfully

Robert G. Barrett

The PERFECT Murder

I was having a drink with some blokes the other night waiting for a band to come on and we were talking about rock'n'roll, venues, bands, etc.

Then we got magging about law and order, the police and naturally enough in the light of things the subject got around to the TRG and SWOS units.

You reckon these blokes didn't have some rotten things to say about what I always thought were a number of dedicated and courageous members of the NSW Police Force?

Gun-crazy yobbos and would-be Rambos they called them.

Trigger-happy psychopaths and misfits who shouldn't even be in the police force let alone be allowed to run around with powerful, dangerous weapons.

Irresponsible bully-boys who get around like they're storm-troopers in a country of occupation. All they're good for is terrorising hippies and greenies because they're easy marks and they can squeeze the girls' tits when they throw them in the back of the police wagon.

Quite frankly, I was amazed. I always thought people had more respect for the TRG boys.

Now there's talk of disbanding the TRG and taking away all their nice, new shotguns with the pistol grips. Well, I disagree with this.

We're talking about a bunch of dedicated men here who have cost the NSW taxpayer a fortune to arm and train, not to mention the effort they have put in on their own unpaid time.

Do you think the curve in the peak of those American-style baseball caps they wear comes made like that? It takes hours to get the right curve in the peaks of those caps like Howard, the lieutenant in *Hill Street Blues*.

How long do you think it takes to be able to fold those blue overalls into those combat boots with the regulation tuck, same as the US Special Forces had in Vietnam?

And what about perfecting that TRG walk after operations? The kevlar helmet in one hand, the shotgun in the other, yet able to conceal your face from the TV cameras and still show enough so the boys will know who it is at the piss-up back at HQ after the latest raid.

Countless nights would have been spent clomping up and down the hallway at home in those combat boots while wives and children tried to get to sleep. It's mental strain all around and they don't get paid for this.

These men go in and do their duty, and now politicians and the media want to crucify them.

No wonder their morale is shattered and they want to go on strike. And some smarties say 'good'. At least a few innocent people will be safe in their homes for a while.

All these blokes really need is a bit of good PR and some proper marketing.

I used to write a bit of copy on radio and a few ads. If they want to be like the Yanks, why not go for it all the way?

The first thing I'd piss off is those names. TRG — that always reminds me of Roy Rogers calling for his horse. And SWOS — fair dinkum, who thought that up? It could stand for Sewerage, Waste, Offal and Sludge and sounds like something you clean bathrooms with.

How about: The NSW Police Force Death's Head Commando Battalion? The NSW Police Force Ranger Attack Unit? The Red Scorpions? Black Tigers? Blue Panthers? Delta Force Blue Mobile Killer Elite? Death From The Doorway …?

But how can I fool my readers? You've probably seen through me already. One week I'm bagging the cops, next thing I'm sucking up to them trying to curry favour. Just another media sycophant. And you're half-right too.

It's just that I saw a way to commit the perfect murder. Kill someone and get off scot-free. Say there was some bastard out there you didn't like: a bank manager or someone who owes you money and won't settle; a panelbeater, a builder or a drug dealer who's ripped you off.

You ring up the TRG. Some constable answers the phone.

You say: 'There's a bloke out there, Charlie Dunk of such and such a street, so and so. He's a drug dealer, he's got a gun, he's a gibbering psychopath who hates cops and he reckons all TRG blokes sit down to piss. He's a menace to society, he's half-Abo and he's out on bail. Go get the mother. Do it, do it, go, go, go. Yay team!'

The following night sit back, relax, watch a bit of TV. Make a nice toasted cheese sandwich and a mug of Ovaltine.

Then go to bed and get a good night's sleep happy in the knowledge that at 2.30 a.m. the Tactical Response Group's gonna smash the bastard's door down, thunder up the stairs in combat boots armed with shotguns, kick his bedroom door in and scream, 'You on the #%*@!% bed. Don't move or ... BLAM! BLAM! BLAM! BANG! KA-BLAM! POW! We'll blow your #@*%!% head off!'

KILL two birds with ONE STONE

There are a number of problems facing Australia today, two of which are drugs and Aboriginal drinking.

As soon as you mention 'Aboriginal drinking problem' the Kooris get the hump.

But if you saw *60 Minutes* a few weeks ago, the evidence was there in graphic and horrifying detail.

There was an Aboriginal woman in hospital for the umpteenth time getting her head stitched. She'd previously been in with broken arms and legs and assorted injuries her husband inflicted on her when he was drunk.

There was film of an Aboriginal man bashing his wife in a riverbed with a piece of wood. When he got sick of hitting her he started throwing rocks at her. He was drunk, too.

Several Aboriginal men got up on camera and admitted they bashed their wives because they went mad on the drink.

Then there was a moving scene of Aboriginal women from all over the NT, in body paint, marching down the main street of Alice Springs protesting about the bashings and growing alcoholism.

So the Kooris can get the hump all they want but the proof was there. And the bottom line is, they can't handle booze; it's not in their nature.

They got on quite well for scores of thousands of years before the whites introduced them to it.

Now on to the drug problem. Where do you start and what drug? Heroin addicts robbing banks and breaking into houses?

People shoving cars, houses and bank accounts up their nose to support a cocaine habit?

Kids, 16, shooting speed and getting free needles to do so from their nearest drug counselling centre? Schoolkids getting out of it on Rohypnol and Serepax?

Weightlifters shooting anabolic steroids? People popping ecstasy at dance parties and discos?

LSD, peyote, mescaline, boiled cane toads, angel's trumpets, magic mushrooms? Cough medicine, aeroplane glue? Cigarettes, alcohol? The new ones — ice and crack? And, of course, the old favourite, marijuana?

Where do you start? We're definitely a drug-prone society and it's increasing. I'm convinced of one thing — the lesser of all the drug evils is pot. Not that filling your lungs with smoke can be any good for you.

But I've still never heard of anyone dying from an overdose of smoking pot. You can only take so much.

King Kong couldn't smoke four Buddha sticks and half a bag of Queensland heads. He'd end up looking like 20 tonnes of Scottish haddock, waking up every couple of hours saying, 'Hey man, play the other side of that album.'

When Sydney footballers were drug-tested and registered positive to pot, the furore and breast-beating from the league and a few holier-than-thou sports commentators was unbelievable.

As Sydney solicitor Chris Murphy succinctly put it: 'The league is sponsored by beer and cigarettes. I challenge any doctor to tell me pot is any worse.' Not a bad point, Chris.

They can fill the gaols to bursting point like they're doing but they're not going to stop people scrounging up a smoke. And as for gaol and rehabilitation — a mate of mine did three years for pot and the first thing he did on release was buy a bag of pot with his gaol money. He did it deliberately.

There was a photo in the local rag of the NSW Police Commissioner under the heading, 'Police Commissioner With Drug Haul'. There he was, po-faced, holding a plastic bag with about half-a-dozen foils in it. A few lousy grams of crappy leaf.

And while he was posing for the cameras with this massive drug haul, about another 20kg of heroin lobbed into the country.

The speed and ecstasy factories are going into overtime. Kids are dying and some high-flyer probably brings in another 5kg of coke under diplomatic immunity.

Judges argue about lessening the penalties for pot but politicians can't make up their minds, only because they'd put their grandmothers in gaol if they thought there was a vote in it.

So, as a concerned citizen and taxpayer, I thought I might take a punt and put up a suggestion to ease both the drug and the Aboriginal drinking problems.

Why not let the Aborigines, if they wish to, run the marijuana industry?

Now before the zealots surround my house with burning torches and wooden stakes, let's have a look at this radical and outrageous proposition purely from a financial point of view.

I don't know how much pot is sold in NSW. With all these sensational, multi-million-dollar drug crops it's impossible to tell. But let's settle on a nice round sum, say $20 million a year. Let the Kooris grow pot out in the country under strict supervision and sell it at a regulated price.

They cop half the $20 million. The rest is a two-way whack-up between the State and Federal Governments.

Why don't we give it a trial run for two years?

Throw in plenty of bureaucratic red tape, like you have to be 21 and working to buy a bag and you can't buy more than two ounces at a time. And if anybody apart from a Koori is caught selling pot, then it's off to the pokey for some severe questioning.

Besides the money, look at the other benefits. The poor old smoker would be happy and have a much better rapport with the police. I'm sure the cops must be sick of arresting and alienating people who would prefer to be on their side, just so they can win votes for their political masters.

And with the extra $10 million a year going towards the police and customs, they could concentrate on the heroin and cocaine trade and jump on the importers, instead of a few hippies and ordinary working people.

The Kooris would have to be happy. They'd be $10 million in front, off welfare and off the piss.

And what are Aborigines, especially the elders, good at? Painting. And what's pot good for? Enhancing creativity in the arts.

Imagine all those Kooris cashed up and not getting so drunk, doing beautiful bark paintings of Thugine the rainbow snake,

Mulloka the water devil, Bohrah the kangaroo. Churning them out, happy as clams. Another million-dollar spin-off industry.

I discussed this with a couple of other drunks in a pub and they looked at me through bleary eyes and hailed the idea as genius. I don't know about that.

But, after watching *60 Minutes*, it just struck me as a much nicer and more profitable way for the Aboriginal men to stone their wives.

CROSS my HEART and hope to DIET

In the time I've been writing this column I doubt if anyone can say I've used it to score freebies.

The old payola. You know — eat at so-and-so's restaurant, buy a car from such-and-such motors, drink brand X bourbon.

When it comes to scoring freebies I'm a failure. In fact, the only things I've rapped have been two Australian books — which I set out to roast and it backfired on me. And I gave a nudist resort a rap because it backfired on the editor.

Apart from that and Greenpeace I don't think I've had a kind word to say about anything or anybody.

But this week's column is going to be a walking, talking, non-stop free advertisement for a book. A blatant and outrageous free plug. Ah-ha, you say. He's finally succumbed. What's the miserable bastard getting out of this?

The answer is: nothing. Zilch. Not a cracker. I didn't write the book. It wasn't even written by an Australian – two Americans wrote it. Worst of all, I actually forked out $9.95 for it.

So what's in it for yours truly? I'm doing it because of my feelings for my lovely readers.

I doubt if there are many people out there who don't have a bit of a weight problem.

Fair enough, all the girls can't look like Elle Macpherson and the blokes can't look like Jimmy Thunder.

But there aren't too many around who wouldn't miss a few kilos. And I'm no exception.

I'm telling you I've tried everything to lose weight. I've run, swum, paddled skis, surfed.

I've worked out in gyms till I've almost collapsed. Gone to aerobics classes and farted in front of twenty housewives.

I've tried the Israeli army diet, the Pritikin diet, the Auschwitz rotten cabbage diet. I've lived on speed for days at a time till I ended up talking like Donald Duck and watched the furniture grow legs and chase me around the loungeroom.

I'd lose weight, then put it all back on a week later. I was fit enough with a good heartbeat and low blood pressure, but I still looked like a walrus.

Then one day I bumped into two old mates who'd been living in the country for a while and who I barely recognised when I did. And they tipped me to this book. They said it would change my life.

And believe me, baby, it has. It's called *Fit for Life*. It's written by two Seppos, Harley and Marilyn Diamond. It's published by Angus&Robertson and it's ten bucks, less a zack, so there.

It's not a diet book and it's not an exercise book. It's a book of plain common-bloody-sense, plus a few discoveries. Yet it's that simple you wonder why somebody didn't twig to it before.

There are twenty-four hours in a day, which breaks down to eight three-hour periods. The book more or less explains what you can and what you can't do in those eight-hour periods.

And it's also based on a thing called 'personal hygiene'. Which I might add has nothing to do with my rotten breath, cheesy toes or woofy armpits.

The first week I started on this thing I thought I'd gained five kilograms and caught pneumonia. My stomach bloated up, my nose was running like a tap, my eyes were sore and my ears rang. Some #@%*%! book, I thought.

Then I read on and found out my miserable body was detoxifying itself. It's not only fat we're carrying around. It's the kilograms of poisons, preservatives and other crap we've accumulated over the years.

Think of all those lovely pizzas, pies, cheeseburgers, chocolate malteds, sausage sandwiches, Chiko rolls, etc., we've stuffed down our screeches over the years. Not counting coffee, cigarettes and booze.

The remnants of all this is in our system along with the blubber. You've got to get rid of it. And this book tells you how to do that without killing yourself or going hungry. It's all that easy and simply explained it makes you blink.

Anyway, enough of this. I'm getting hungry and I have to go and cook lunch.

Today I'm having a nice, big, juicy T-bone steak with heaps of grouse fresh vegetables covered in melted butter.

Yesterday I had six steamed dim-sims from this little Thai takeaway place.

Bugger going on a diet.

I'd rather lose weight permanently and stay … *Fit for Life*.

Casey's WAGE isn't WON

I don't know whether anyone else in Australia knows, or is even interested, that in Sydney there's a radio announcer by the name of Ron Casey.

Ron had the temerity to speak out on air about Australia's stuffed-up immigration policy, during which he made one or two mildly disparaging remarks about Asians.

This now appears tantamount to a capital offence in Australia for anyone who's white, was born here and has an Anglo-Saxon name.

Casey is the new whipping-boy for the anti-discrimination board, the ethnic affairs department and the ever holier-than-thou-anti-racist mob that's sick of putting the boot into Bruce

Ruxton because too many people were listening to him and he made too much sense.

I've only ever listened to Casey's show for a few minutes here and there. It's ordinary.

He's a boring, droning, one-eyed wombat with about as much sense of humour as a Dalek.

But I don't believe he's a racist.

Not that I'd give a stuff anyway. But I'm trying to think what all the kerfuffle is that got ethnic affairs wanting to draw and quarter him and feed his carcass to the vultures.

Evidently, an upset housewife rang him one day and had a beef about a meal she had in Chinatown. She claimed the food was awful and the waiters were dropkicks who treated her like a pig and said untoward things about Australians.

Casey sympathised with the woman and said when that happens you feel like going back with some friends and kicking over a few tables and chairs. Let them know you're not quite as dim as you sim. Casey's idea of a joke.

But for these comments he was forced off the air by the ethnic affairs mob who wanted him hung on the spot. It's a wonder in this climate of multiculturalism they didn't want to cut off his hand or call for a public beheading!

He got back on air — after the ethnic affairs team spent about half-a-million dollars of taxpayers' money on QCs and barristers to try to keep him off.

Then some old digger rang him on Anzac Day for a whinge about the Japs and what they did to him and his mates when he was a POW.

The Irish in Casey got the better of him and he went into bat for the old digger, echoing his sentiments about the Japanese being cruel, heartless, barbaric little bastards. And the ethnic affairs mob screamed again.

Casey said it wouldn't hurt if migrants learnt to speak English when they get here. More discriminatory and racist remarks, came the howl from the ethnic affairs team.

Yet the mayor of Darwin — a Chinese–Aussie — said exactly the same thing on TV the other night. But he's not a white Australian so he's allowed to do this.

Casey's latest outburst concerns the newest boatload of Cambodians to decide to jump the immigration queue. Casey reckoned they should be put on a cattle boat and sent back with 'Australian Reject' stamped on them.

I suppose that lacks tack, but in a way he's got a point.

Do you know it costs us millions each year to fly illegal immigrants back to wherever they came from? And some of them go first class!

Like: 'Bad luck they wouldn't let you into Australia, sir.'

'Thank you, steward …'

Hawke let 20,000 Chinese students enter in one hit that will cost us another $30m a year in social security benefits — and most of them were here illegally in the first place.

We can't find the money to fix the salinity problem in our rivers.

We have to flog our forests off to the Japs to make into cardboard boxes and John Williamson has to pass the hat round after his concerts to try to find $40,000 to save our koalas.

We're being shafted from within and without and they haven't even got the decency to use a bit of Vaseline.

But for sheer arrogance in treating us like mugs, you have to give it to the Japs. They told Greenpeace Australia that they were a bunch of racists for trying to stop the bastards' whaling industry — because whaling was a Japanese tradition.

And Japanese multinational Daikyo, which owns half of Cairns, has sponsored some sporting team they're calling the Daikyo Dolphins.

Can you believe it? After the bastards indiscriminately slaughter more than two million dolphins a year with their driftnets?

Even the arch-villain of radio, 2UE's John Laws — the mongrel — mentioned it in his newspaper column under the title 'It's Time To End This Migrant Rort'; he wrote about the 11,000 so-called Chinese businessmen who came here and now the government doesn't even know where they are. They arrive, buy a house, then piss off back to Hong Kong to keep wheeling and dealing.

Laws mentioned the migrant family reunion program, where a migrant can come to Australia then bring his mum, dad, grandpa, grandma and all the aunts and uncles … and they go straight on the pension — which we all pay for!

Yet a Vietnam veteran suffering from cancer caused by the war can't even get a disability pension!

Ron Casey mentions things like this and the ethnic affairs mob have him taken off the air.

Yet every letter to the editor I've read lately is on his side.

Like I said, to me, Ron Casey is a bore and a pain in the arse and I wouldn't listen to him in the morning if you held a gun to my head. But he's certainly got his finger on the pulse of public opinion.

And these ethnic affairs lobby groups pillory him for what is nothing more than having a colourful — if slightly insensitive — way of telling the bloody truth.

If you ask me, it's wrong.

JAWS 5: The Butcher takes off

A column written by Paul Kidd, called *Wobbegong Songs*, brought a Barrett incident to mind so, without trying to steal Paul's thunder, I thought I might do a sort of fishing column.

There's no doubt Paul's column isn't half-bad, although I don't know about this character he's dredged up — 'No Knees Norton'.

You don't take the name Norton in vain, not where I'm concerned anyway.

But to the point. I like to go fishing — not angling. I couldn't for the life of me stand on some rocky headland, freezing my nuts off for hours on end. Or spend half a day lurching up and down in a leaky boat, breathing in diesel fumes and rotten fish guts while I spewed my heart up.

I like to go spearfishing — get in, get a feed and get out again. And although I'm a dedicated greenie and peacenik, I see nothing wrong at all with getting a speargun and blowing some fish's brains out, then flaying it, ripping its guts out and tossing it in a pan.

Love and Krishna are very nice, but bream fillets in tarragon and white wine sauce are absolutely beautiful.

This story goes back to when I was a pimply-faced, 17-year-old apprentice butcher at Bondi. Forget about Saddam Hussein, the Butcher of Baghdad. I was Bob Barrett, the Butcher of Bondi.

We used to go spearfishing most afternoons after work. In those days the murk wasn't so bad and as long as it blew off-shore the water would be reasonably clear.

The fish always seemed to come in just on dusk to feed — mainly morwong, Tassie trumpeters, drummer etc.

This particular arvo I was with two mates, Grant Joss and Johnny Sutton.

Now the idea with spearfishing is the first bloke in on his own generally gets a fish. I told Grant and John they'd been getting a heap of flathead on the sand just down from the boatsheds, so they jumped in at the boatramps while smartarse Barrett, the Butcher of Bondi, jumped in further around at a spot we called the Flat Rock.

Thought I'd knock over a couple of fish while my two mates wasted their time swimming over the sand looking for non-existent flathead. I've always been a good bloke like that.

It was calm, low tide, a little cloudy for February and the water wasn't all that clear. But apart from a school of trevally, there wasn't a fish to be seen.

I thought this was a little curious as I snorkelled on. I was barely 20 metres out and about five metres down and there was no sign of fish.

I dived down again, came up and just where I'd dived was the biggest $#@%*! shark I had ever seen. It had a nose on it wider than a '63 Cadillac, was six metres long if it was a centimetre and no more than four metres away.

I'll never forget the bastard as long as I live. It had all these stripes running down it and dozens of tiny fish swimming in front of its mouth.

It was a tiger shark.

I just floated there for a moment looking at it and automatically pointed my gun at it as it rose off the bottom towards me.

Then this voice seemed to say: 'Oh, Bob Barrett, Butcher of Bondi, that speargun's gonna be about as much use with a shark that size as a Violet Crumble bar in a knife fight.'

But I didn't panic. I just dropped the speargun, turned and made that 20 metres back to shore in about four seconds flat, leaving a cloud of shit behind me Superman couldn't see through. It was low tide but I went straight up those rocks like a coconut crab.

A couple of blokes fishing on the rocks looked more horrified than me when this thing suddenly materialised in front of them as if Scotty had beamed it down from the Enterprise. I was shaking like a leaf and whiter than goat's milk. I couldn't even get the words out.

'Mark! Spark! Blark!' I was spluttering it out to Grant and John who were now snorkelling over to where I'd been — I might have stolen the jump on them as far as the fish went but I wasn't about to watch them get eaten.

They finally saw me jumping around like a baboon, swum over and got out of the water. Of course, by now there was no sign of the shark. So it was on.

'Bewdy Bob. Saw a big shark, did you?' Scorn, ridicule. 'Onya, Barrett. Frightened by your own shadow.' Guffaw, bleah.

I yelled out to the boardriders in the north corner to get out of the water and who should come paddling over but Bernie Morton, son of the late Tex Morton, the singer.

Bernie was an argumentative dropkick who would start a fight in an empty house. He loved rubbishing me and today was his day.

He retrieved my speargun, which was still floating where I'd left it, and gave me another blast. There was still no sign of the shark. As he paddled off, his parting words were, 'Barrett's probably seen a wobbegong'.

He was heading towards the beach when we all yelled out, 'Bernie, behind you!' He turned around and there was this fin sticking nearly two metres out of the water and heading straight for him.

The shark wasn't in the race. Bernie went up the rocks like a torpedo and I reckon he was halfway to Dover Heights before he stopped running.

We all stood on the rocks and watched that tiger shark ripping the school of trevally to pieces till it got dark. We reckoned it was at least six metres long — a monster.

How it didn't take me, I'll never know. Someone must have been in my corner that February afternoon.

SNOWED under

Sex, glamour, raging — but no TAB.

Remember my mate Steve the chef and how I took him to the opening of that nudist resort at Port Stephens and how we both had a top day? He's just returned the favour. And I had a wonderful time in the snowfields with him and the Snow Toad. A perfect pair.

Steve cracked it as a chef at the White Spider restaurant in the Eiger Chalet at Perisher Valley. All very swish. Get myself down there, free food and accommodation, ski as much as I like, just say I was one of the staff — a kitchen hand.

I'd never seen snow let alone stayed in a chalet. But I knew it was full-on glamour, beautiful women, non-stop partying and it cost a fortune. And here I had it on a plate.

My bus rolled into Perisher around 4.30 p.m. to five metres of snow and five below zero. Steve met me and we walked across to the Eiger just as about 400 drunks on skis burst out of The Man From Snowy River pub.

I'd arrived just in time for the finish of some cross-country, pub-to-pub drunken ski-a-thon. So much for the sophistication and glamour.

Then Steve showed me my 'free' accommodation. The room was a bit smaller than a cell in Long Bay with two bunks and about enough room for a Munchkin on the floor: which looked like where I was gonna sleep.

Luckily the bloke sharing with Steve had a sheila in tow so I got the top bunk. I hired gear so I'd look the part. I was still trying to figure out what this white stuff on the ground was.

Next, dinner and meet the staff, including the Snow Toad, Tracy. I used to work in a restaurant in Terrigal with Tracy where she was called the Terrigal Toad. Now she's known as the Snow Toad. For a waitress she always reminded me of one of The Belles Of St Trinians.

Steve didn't tell me he was also the breakfast cook. I was snoring my head off when this buzzer went off and I heard Steve abusing somebody in the room. Hello, I thought, we've got a burglar. But no, it was only Steve with the choke out revving himself up to go to work.

I decided to catch up on some sleep — next thing, snow wagons and skidoos started roaring past the window. It sounded like Phillip Island on ice. Worse.

After an hour I gave up and tackled breakfast. It was beautiful outside so I went for a walk in all my snow gear to check the place out.

I trudged and sloshed up and down in the snow twisting my knees, stuffing-up my legs and starting to wonder what I was doing. I persevered for a while but besides it giving me the shits, my feet felt like they were stuck in two rabbit traps and my thighs felt as if I'd lost three rounds of Thai-boxing. I was about to hit the top bunk when Steve informed me I was on at 5.30 p.m.

'What the @#%$* on?' I asked.

A kitchen hand cracked a bone in his arm skiing and I was going to do a shift in the kitchen.

I couldn't believe it. I'd had no sleep for two nights, my feet and legs were absolutely killing me — plus I was half-pissed. Now I looked like doing six hours over a steaming sink. So much for my free ride in the snow.

I threw the towel in at 10.30. They could sack me for all I cared. I needed a night in a kitchen about as much as Peter Garrett needs hair conditioner.

Still in my hire gear I had a few more bourbons then trudged across to 'The Man' to do a complete job on myself.

Next morning Steve abused the same bloke at 6.30 a.m. The skidoos started up shortly after. I crawled down to the kitchen still in the hire gear, pigged out, bought a paper and checked the form.

Here I discovered two things: firstly, going skiing is as much a pose as it is a sport. You have to be seen in the right outfit, carrying the right skis and bindings, with the right sunglasses and headband. All preferably imported from Finland or Austria. The idea is to hit the slopes looking as much like a rainbow lorikeet as possible.

Secondly, I figured out why I had the tom-tits. It wasn't just lack of sleep, the cold, the fact I couldn't ski to save my life and that I was going to have to work in a kitchen. There's no TAB down there.

I was into my third day of not having a bet and going through bad withdrawal. And all I could see in the paper were good things to back.

Another day of no punting and no sleep and I'd finish in the rathouse. It was time to haul arse.

I told Steve work had called and I had to get back quickly. What a bummer and I was having such a good time.

Just for a change I got drunk in the evening and mushed off with Steve across the frozen wastes to the pub to finish the job.

Forget this rattle about snowbunnies. The pub was full of blokes. If Roseanne Barr walked in some bloke would've thrown her up in the air. A girl working at the chalet reckoned it was one of the best years she'd ever had in the snow for bonking.

So I had about as much chance of getting a root as Woody Allen going three rounds with Mike Tyson.

Somehow, despite blokes in bulk, the Toad still missed out. So she gave me and Steve a gobful as she left. 'All men are *#@%$! no good #@%*@'s! Including you two.' Okay Toad. If you say so.

Steve and I weaved our way back to the chalet, drank whatever we could get our hands on then rolled into our bunks. And that was Saturday night.

Steve abusing the invisible man and the skidoos woke me up again. Despite a roaring hangover I didn't mind. The Uncle Gus left at 8.30 a.m., I pigged out again, thanked Steve for a spiffing time and said I'd see him back at Terrigal.

I was happier to be home than a hunchback who's just seen someone with a bigger hunch.

Terrigal may not have the glamour of the snowfields — life in the fast lane there is the eight-items-or-less checkout counter at Food Barn — but I've got a bed and at least there's a TAB.

Better a WHITE racist bastard than a BLACK

Some time ago I did a bit of a hatchet job on Alan Jones in this column — mainly about his views on environmental issues.

A lot of people out there who reckon I'm a 25-carat turd and would like to see me boiled in rancid sump oil, still agree with what I say on occasions. The same with Alan Jones.

He wrote an excellent column in the *Sun-Herald* about Africa and the hypocrisy of Western nations when it comes to pandering to a lot of tin-pot black African dictators and the applying of sanctions and embargoes against South Africa.

The truth in Jones' column appears every night on TV with the news coming out of South Africa and surrounding states — even on the ABC, which has the most biased version of events happening in South Africa imaginable.

So far around 1000 blacks have been butchered in South Africa by their own people.

If you did to an animal what they do to each other a judge would give you 20 years. Nothing as quick and simple as shooting each other in the head. They swarm onto a train and hack women and children to pieces with machetes.

They go into a town or workers' barracks, drag the people out, pour petrol over them and burn them alive. All in the name of freedom and equality for my black brothers and sisters.

Even Winnie Mandela has been charged as an accessory to the murder of some kid called Stompy who was beaten to a pulp then had his throat cut. He was barely 14.

Yet whenever the ANC or whatever come out here the grandstanding bleeding hearts can't get down and kiss their backsides quick enough.

And no-one knows how much of our money Bonzer Bob has given them in aid. Probably millions.

I reckon the day the blacks get majority rule in South Africa there'll be a bloodbath that will make what the Japs did during the siege of Nanking look like the festival of Aquarius in Nimbin.

The only thing that can help to stop it is the white government.

They're far from perfect and I don't think I could ever see myself getting into a shout with a bunch of those Afrikaners, but I believe they're the ones we should be giving aid to, not bunging sanctions on them.

The communists must be laughing their heads off while they wait in the wings rubbing their hands with glee.

And if the blacks do take over in South Africa, who will they model their style of government on? Bob Mugabe in Zimbabwe? It's a corrupt dictatorship where offenders in the government are pardoned and dissenters are shot.

What about the new bunch of jolly chaps that have just taken over in Liberia? In one incident alone they herded 600 women and kids into a church and killed the lot. The bodies were stacked almost 2m deep.

Some bloke called Bongo just built a $120m church and the Pope came out and blessed it. The people are starving and they have hardly any hospitals.

In Somalia 60,000 civilians have been murdered. Mengistu Haile Mariam in Ethiopia? He sent the troops in to machine-gun several hundred starving peasant farmers because they asked for land reform and something for their starving kids to eat.

In the Sudan they cut off your right hand if you break a minor law and if you crack it for a dropkick of a break they cut your foot off as well.

How about Idi Amin?

Maybe he could come out of retirement in Saudi Arabia or where ever he's holed up with all the loot he snaffled out of Uganda and take up a post as some sort of government advisor.

What about Ken Kuanda in Zambia? He was a big hit with Bonzer and the team at the CHOGM conference when he demanded power-sharing for the blacks in South Africa, yet if you try to form an opposition party in Zambia they take you out and put you in front of a firing squad.

Fascinating lot, aren't they?

And there's no shortage of punters to choose from. Out of 51 African states only six allow their people to hold elections and choose their leaders, yet they're all members of the United Nations. It's got me stuffed.

It wouldn't surprise me if some grungy dyke working in the ABC read this and said, 'That racist bastard. He ought to be castrated'.

Well that's more than fine by me. I'd much rather be a white racist bastard living in Australia than a black in South Africa. Out here they only cut off my orchestras, which haven't been that much use to me anyway.

Over there I'd be necklaced.

A McCullough to CUT the DEADWOOD

I would like to take my hat off to a lady. 'Lady' has taken an awful battering in Australia lately; there are no sheilas, birds, chicks, etc. left in Oz, they're all referred to as ladies now.

And the lady in question smokes, loves a drink and has a laugh that would knock the icing off a wedding cake at 10 metres.

I'm convinced if she heartily enjoyed a baked dinner she would not be adverse to breaking wind at the dinner table. But in this miserable chauvinist's eyes she is still every inch a lady.

I refer to author Colleen McCullough. Possibly the best writer this country's ever produced.

A writer is only as good as how many books he or she sells.

Colleen's *The Thorn Birds* sold 10.5 million alone. Yet her peers and literary review boards pooh-pooh her and say she's not a good writer. She's vulgar and plebeian and her works aren't literature. In other words she writes books normal people can understand and enjoy, and makes a packet while she's at it.

She doesn't come up with a lot of boring elitist shit that goes over everybody's head, except of course the literary elite.

Has anybody out there ever come across a literary elite? Has anybody out there ever come across a literary review board?

If you were washed up on a desert island with six members of a literary review board and a tin of corned beef, you'd kill and eat the literary review board and keep the tin of corned beef for the act of social intercourse.

The same with the authors they support. They're the most boring, procrastinating, self-opinionated drones imaginable and half of them couldn't write their name on a brasco door.

I sprung Colleen McCullough letting go with one of her laughs at these drones on *The 7.30 Report*. When asked the secret of her success, she replied that she didn't consider herself all that great a writer, but she simply wrote to give people enjoyment and not to impress the literary elite, particularly in this country.

No wonder she's laughing all the way to the bank. Yet these ponces she's referring to swan around in their tweed coats and skivvies or overalls and shirts, come up with a binder full of bathroom mould that would be lucky if it sold 1000 copies and consider themselves the literary elite.

If they were writing for a feed you wouldn't give them a paper plate. Yet they all live quite well thank you on handouts from the literature board. A glorified writer's dole.

I know one writer who's milked almost $250,000 from the Literature Board and every two years he comes up with 150 pages of 25-carat horseshit that no-one can understand. You read one of his books and you feel like going out to the garage, getting your Black and Decker and drilling a hole in your head to see if you're still alive. Yet the wine-and-cheese mob gush over it and say, 'Marvellous, simply marvellous'.

I'm not against grants. I got a small one myself once. But I swear I'd written two books off my own bat before I knew the rort was on and found out how to apply. And I'm eternally grateful to the Arts Council for getting me out of the steamy kitchens for six months to write another book in moderate comfort. I get letters from housewives and punters with definite talent asking me how to crack it as a writer in Australia. And I'll state categorically there's got to be a fairer and more equitable way of handing out these grants where budding writers can get half a go and not just the same bunch of greedy, selfish bores year in and year out.

I reckon everyone in Australia should be entitled to $15,000 once, to take a year off to write a book. Providing they've had something published off their own bat, be it a bit of poetry, an article or a short story or whatever to prove they can use a typewriter and have the ability to write.

Christ! With $15,000 tax-free sitting in the bank and doing a bit of casual work on the side, if you couldn't come up with a 300-page novel in 12 months you should be stuffed and have your clothes burnt.

If this were adopted, I'm convinced there would be a resurgence of writing in this country like you wouldn't believe.

And we could get rid of all that deadwood with their snouts stuck firmly in the Literature Board trough.

Unfortunately, at present, due to a mad hatter's tea party of toffee-nosed elitists, it ain't going nowhere like that.

But, to the 503 that missed out on a grant and any others out there trying to get a book together: don't get too discouraged by all this waffle going on around you.

If an overweight woman with a laugh that would split a railway sleeper can make millions (and an ex-butcher who's going that bald you can almost read his mind can make a reasonable living), you can do it.

Unfortunately, you're going to have to forget about the literary elite and write for that detestable, low-life rabble — the general public.

MIKE, I'm not a RACIST ... just BORED

I always do my best to write things that might interest our readers all over Australia.

But occasionally someone in Sydney does such a job on themselves you have to mention it.

I'm talking about Mike Carlton, the radio DJ.

I used to be a regular Mike Carlton listener — when he was funny. He does good voice impersonations and on his day could be reasonably entertaining.

However, Mike's not short of ego, as he once mentioned on TV, and he can also be a moralising, self-opinionated bore that would empty a bar giving away free piss.

He's embraced the feminist cause and he's right up there on the anti-racism witch-hunt-cum-bandwagon rolling around the country.

Mike's two favourite whipping persons are the Meadow Lea margarine TV commercial — it's sexist — and, of course, South Africa.

But no matter what, Mike 'ought to be, con-grad-u-lated'. He did win an award in Melbourne for radio excellence called Raywards. I only wish I was talented enough to win something like that myself.

Mike was waffling away over the cornflakes on 2GB and rating fairly well about the same time 'the mongrel', John Laws, split for 2UE.

Enter Jane Singleton to take over Lawsie's spot. If you think Carlton can be boring, Singleton is the industrial-strength version. Once ensconced at the station she got into Carlton's ear and they both decided they were going to be the new moral conscience of Australia as far as racism goes.

And away these two shining lights went — boring the tits off whatever listeners 2GB had left after Lawsie legged it.

The Japanese were really greenies with the wellbeing of Australia at heart and never committed any war crimes. There were no Hong Kong triads smuggling heroin into Australia using Vietnamese criminals already living here. The sun absolutely shone out of Nelson Mandela and his comrades in the ANC's backsides etc., etc.

Week after week they droned, putting the boot into all the regulars: the RSL, Casey, Ruxton and Blainey. Any Australian with even a semblance of national pride who thought differently was a jingoistic fascist.

The sad thing is, it's people like Carlton and Singleton on these self-righteous, holier-than-thou, ego-trips that stir up most of the dissension in Australia — migrants or otherwise.

Naturally, most people turned off in droves. Their ratings went down like Linda Lovelace and before long the 2GB executives were that far back in the doghouse they were feeding them with a shanghai.

They gave Jane the flick leaving Carlton to carry the can. Back in the ashes of what was once a reasonably well-rating program Mike offered to resign. But he stayed on.

Such bravery does deserve an award.

I'd like to give him an award for bleating to the papers, after boring his listeners senseless: 'Oh well, if I have to lose a few racists it doesn't worry me.'

In other words, if you change stations because some DJ is giving you GBH of the earhole you're automatically a member of the Ku Klux Klan.

Another award for saying after Laws left: 'Oh well, at least I don't have to prop up John Laws any more.'

While Mike was going down like the *Lusitania* the mongrel went to number one and managed to drag the rest of 2UE up with him.

And he deserves an award for his efforts during the bicentenary and the re-enactment of the First Fleet landing — the so-called Tall Ships. Or as some call it … 'Invasion Day'.

The Tall Ships got torpedoed around Brazil and the NSW Government pulled out because it was turning into a rort with money being wasted everywhere.

Mike rallied the 2GB listeners to cough up over a million bucks and they managed to get the Tall Ships here on time. Mike's quid pro quo was to come when he sailed down Sydney Harbour on the *Soren Larsen* sprouting platitudes about the majesty of it all while everybody told him how wonderful he was.

Talk about a waste of money. Along with the Tall Ships the NSW Government at the time blew more millions on a fireworks display that went up in a blaze of gunpowder and under-developed film.

What about the Bicentennial asthma research centre, a koala sanctuary or a home for the underprivileged kids or the elderly? At least we'd still have something to show for it.

No. Give them bread and circuses.

Funnily enough, while Mike was swanning down the harbour, not far away was the *Our Svanen* with an ad for one of the biggest selling drinks in South Africa right across the sail — Mainstay Rum. It's a product of Mauritius but, as anyone knows, South Africa has heaps of business investments on that island.

I wonder if … No! That couldn't possibly be right.

I don't give a stuff if they drink Mainstay in South Africa or North Korea. Mike said I'm a racist for switching off so I went out and bought a few bottles. And I reckon it's the best white rum going around. It's got everything it says on the label. Absolute clarity and perfect dryness. And don't it get you pissed?

Yo-ho-ho me racist hearties.

Hang on... I was only JOKING

The way it is in Australia lately — with all the politicians pandering to some ethnic vote or other — it's almost impossible to crack a joke or take the piss without offending someone. Especially if you're a white Australian with an Anglo-Saxon name.

It's as if politicians want to turn us into a bunch of humourless drones not game to laugh at ourselves any more. Laugh at someone or something and immediately the moralising do-gooders and pressure groups are calling you racist, fascist, sexist or whatever.

If you said Charles Manson was a typical Scorpio, you'd be a zodicist!

I always thought true Australians were known for their larrikin sense of humour. The old ANZAC thing of laughing at ourselves, and pomposity and absurdities around us.

Take the Australian navy doing a tour of duty in the Persian Gulf.

After weeks of being bored shitless on a stinking hot ship, a few wags got done up as Arabs in Bedouin headgear and bowed towards the nearest oil refinery — taking the piss out of the situation they were in and the pressure they were under.

And what happens? The Arabs couldn't start jumping up and down quick enough, screaming that all Islam had been grossly offended.

They've got to be kidding. They can come to Australia, find religious freedom to build mosques just about wherever they like and then bring some Mullah out. They can brawl among themselves in public and threaten to kill any TV crews sent to cover it. Then they can march down the street burning the Australian flag.

I reckon that's not only offensive, it's downright criminal!

But hardly anybody says a word. Maybe if the Arabs learnt to laugh at themselves they wouldn't be so full of hatred for the infidels.

Though admittedly, they haven't got much to laugh at.

They treat their women as if they're chattels and expect them to get around looking like a cross between Darth Vader and a public letter-box.

They've managed to make Beirut, which was one of the most beautiful cities in the world, look more like the dark side of the moon. And if it weren't for one Arab nation invading another the Australian navy wouldn't be over there.

I reckon our sailors should get a medal for finding something to laugh about in the whole rotten schemozzle.

Another giant drama at the moment surrounds those ads for Hahn beer.

Billboards show an African native with about a metre of copper bands running up his neck. He's holding a bottle of Hahn and saying: 'The first one didn't touch the sides'.

There's another poster of a different native looking like he's got a frisbee jammed in his mouth and he's saying: 'Get your laughing gear around this'.

I reckon they're quite funny and so does the black model who did them — and his family likes it, too. In fact, he's laughing all the way to the bank.

But the do-gooders and holier-than-thou lot all jumped up and screamed it was racist and offensive. And, of course, good ol' Derryn Hinch got in on the act and vowed he'd never drink another bottle of Hahn.

What a load of pious horseshit. If the Labwor or Dodoth tribesmen from the Karamoja or wherever want to get around with their necks resembling a metre of drainpipe and their mouths looking like they're trying to swallow a hubcap, surely we can take the piss a bit without the Hinches of this world and their ilk trying to score brownie points.

I mean, if the ads showed a black bloke on the end of a rope surrounded by ranting idiot rednecks in sheets and the black bloke saying: 'I've been hanging out for a Hahn all day', I'd certainly consider that a bit off.

However, even I admit we do have to draw the line somewhere.

A very disturbing story arrived on my desk this week that I consider highly offensive, from where else but that vilest racist regime — South Africa.

It concerns a white South African doctor with a practice in Durban and a black woman, complaining of a sore throat, who went to see this racist, Afrikaner bastard.

The poor woman was Ugandan and she wasn't just black. She was super black. Almost blue-black. Proud black.

The South African doctor had a quick look at her throat then said, 'Righto. Take off all your clothes and get down on your hands and knees in the middle of the room.' The woman did as she was told.

The doctor looked at her for a moment or two then said, 'Okay. Now go over in front of the fireplace.' The woman did as she was told and crawled over in front of the fireplace.

'All right,' said the doctor, 'now go over near those pot-plants.' The woman did as she was told.

Then the doctor got her to kneel underneath his oil painting of Cecil Rhodes near the far wall, in front of the venetian blinds, crawl back to the middle of the room and finally back in front of the venetian blinds.

Then he told her to put her clothes back on, had another quick look at her throat and wrote her out a script for some antibiotics.

The woman picked up her prescription, looked at the South African doctor and asked: 'You knew all along all I had was a sore throat. Why did you make me take off all my clothes and embarrass me like that?'

The doctor said: 'I didn't really mean to embarrass you. It's just that I'm getting a leather lounge delivered this afternoon and I was just trying to work out the best place to put it.'

Now that's what I call offensive. But then again, what would you expect from a redneck mob of bastards like those bloody South Africans?

SLEAZE STAYS when the PARTY'S OVER

Sydney's Kings Cross — it's rarely out of the news.

Fred Nile's always vowing to clean it up. Several unfortunate backpackers were burned to death there.

It's been the site of various murders. Whenever Hinch and his ilk in the TV media are stuck for a beat-up they always send a crew up to film the molls, or the street kids or someone spaced out on drugs.

Personally, I always gave the place a wide berth even when I lived in Sydney.

I'm not into shooting up heroin, I'm too lousy to pay for a root, and as for those street kids I'm convinced in most cases a good boot up the arse and 12 months in the army would soon stop them sitting around feeling sorry for themselves.

But every city has its red-light or seedy area. You know what's there and if you don't like it, keep out. Too bad I suppose if you happen to live there, but you can always sell up and move somewhere else — like St Kilda or Fortitude Valley.

Anyway, the Kings Cross Festival was on a couple of weeks back and, as Sunday afternoon on the Central Coast is about as exciting as a bread queue in Russia, I thought I might meander down and take a look.

You never know, I might even find something nice to say about it. Though I declare, equivocally, that if ever I gave anyone or anything a compliment I'd ask for a receipt.

I turned into the main drag smack-bang into the crowds and the action, and believe me there was no shortage of voyeurs like myself.

The first thing that caught my eye was a Salsa band and a whole lot of scantily-dressed couples ripping into some dirty dancing. I managed to elbow some kids and women out of the road and wriggle up to the front. I was about to get a photo of a sensational pair of purple knickers when the band stopped for a break.

I missed out there so I joined the swarming masses.

The crowd was a mixed bunch — pretty much like the stalls cramming the side of the road.

You could get acupuncture and acupressure. Natural perfumes and oils. Super powers — personal powers that bring stability in a world of change. Don't ask me what that is. Shades of the Paddington Bazaar. Heaps of T-shirts. I saw a ripper with 'I Am Not American' written on it in English and the same in Arabic above.

I ended up buying two Fourex T-shirts for a couple of those Seppo sheilas I still write to.

There were the usual trinkets and junk jewellery, sexy lingerie and even bonsai plants.

Good ol' Greenpeace had an information stall. There was a team of Japs sketching people for $10 and a horde of them standing in front of an orange juice machine staring in wide-eyed amazement as the machine split and juiced an orange about every three seconds.

I guess when an orange costs about $6 in Tokyo you could understand why.

And while on the subject of the Japanese ... Wasn't it nice of them to slaughter those 600 dolphins the other week? They are a bunch of bastards, aren't they? But don't worry, they'll be getting theirs this month. And remember. You read it here first.

I didn't notice a heavy police presence as I strolled around — apart from a bunch of Bob Geldof and Sinead O'Connor look-alikes drinking piss near the fountain, where 2MMM had a rock band playing loud enough to be heard at Wompa Gate, the crowd in general was quite well behaved.

There were even some old ladies walking around holding balloons on sticks. I saw a bloke in a snake outfit who I recognised from the TV show *The Money or The Gun*, and shortly after the great man himself, Andrew Denton, zipping through the crowd looking like Mickey Mouse on speed.

I bought another T-shirt and a poster from a charming lady running a stall for the Griffin Theatre. It still didn't seem like the Cross to me though. But I was getting hungry so I thought I'd try the various food stalls.

At the first one some bloke was stirring what looked like a pile of charred ambergris while he smoked a cigarette and the sweat dripped from his nose to sizzle in with whatever it was he was cooking. There were things in it that could have been raisins or, on the other hand, the local rats could have been eating extra well.

I settled for a satay stick at another one and was about to take a bite when, at the back of the stall, I saw his partner sitting in the gutter smoking a cigarette while he poked pieces of chicken or fox terrier on the sticks accompanied by about 6000 flies. I'm not particularly against multiculturalism but I'm definitely against botulism. I ended up buying a kransky on a roll that was so salty if I'd have died from eating it, I reckon I would have been dead six months before my body started to decompose. I brought it up all over some poor bloke retrieving the aluminium cans from a garbage tin. He never knew what hit him. That was enough for me. I hit the toe for the pub where I'd parked my car.

I don't quite know how to sum up the Kings Cross Festival. But one little cameo I saw said it all.

A fresh-faced girl selling plastic flowers while right behind her some moll is propped in a doorway hawking her fork. Artificial flowers. Artificial love. Is there a moral there? I don't know. But it was an aberration that went with my indigestion.

The last HURRAH for BONDI BRAD

I have been to about three funerals in my life. My father's, my grandmother's and the service for a builder on the Central Coast because he and his widow were okay.

Personally, I hate the bloody things. They're even worse than having to go to court. I'd rather be out getting drunk with some mates.

Brad Mayes was one of the most horrible drunks I knew. He was obstreperous, uproarious and the original goodtime Charlie.

He loved to laugh and was one of those rotten types who aren't happy unless they have you laughing too.

I don't know how many times I'd walk into a pub and Brad would have a beer in my hand before I even had a chance to get to the bar. Brad loved a cool one almost as much as he loved his friends.

I grew up with Brad in Bondi.

His father was a legendary sweep from Tamarama Surf Club and surfer from the era when half-a-dozen blokes out at North Bondi was a crowded day.

Jack 'Bluey' Mayes pioneered surfing films in Australia and discovered half the surfing spots up and down the NSW coast that today's surfers take for granted.

Naturally, it rubbed off on Brad. I turned off surfing at Bondi when it started getting too crowded, became a 'lid' and joined Tamarama Surf Club.

Brad powered on and became a champion surfer around Australia in the '70s.

He won a heap of contests and there wouldn't be too many surfers around Australia who didn't know Brad.

Yet the contests weren't all that important to Brad. He just loved to surf. He was one of those weird blokes that would even give you a wave.

Brad hated my books.

Often I was on the end of a clout round the ears, a beer-spilling bearhug or a slap on my sunburned back from the drunken big pest, when he'd spot me in the pub and demand to know why the next one wasn't finished.

There's even a story going round about when he was a beach inspector at Tamarama. He'd got to a good part of *The Godson* and someone ran up and pointed to a poof going out to sea in a rip, screaming his lungs out.

Brad looked up over the railing, nodded and said, 'Yeah I see him. I'll get him as soon as I finish this page.' And continued reading.

Brad was a legend in his own way — a legendary drinker and eater. His numerous surfing treks to Bali and the eight-course meals are legend. A dinner date with Brad was Brad ordering two T-bone steaks for himself, then eating half his girl's too.

And on the social scene everything was giant. You didn't go out for a drink. You went out to get giant. You never woke up with a hangover. You just got too giant the night before. A raging party with music going all night was just simplified as giant. Then you got up the following morning and went out in three-metre surf for two hours.

Of course, all the sheilas hated Brad too. But they always do hate tall, good looking blokes with a ton of personality.

As well as Bondi and Tamarama, Brad was beach inspector at Maroubra.

Then he drifted up to Byron Bay and started shaping surfboards (about the same time as I drifted up to Terrigal and started shaping stories) before he drifted back to Sydney.

After that I'd bump into him and the team every now and again but not as often as I wanted.

To my absolute chagrin though, the last time I saw Brad I played him wide.

He was getting married in Terrigal. He'd met that special person, they were in love and he'd had enough partying and was keen to settle down.

He had work lined up, her parents were giving them a house in Terrigal and things couldn't have looked rosier.

The night I saw him he was in his mate Wally's hot-dog shop in Terrigal.

Brad and his girl were up there getting all the wedding arrangements together.

Naturally, he was a bit giant and as soon as he saw me he started to roar.

After getting belted I backpedalled out, said I had to meet a mate upstairs in the bar and I'd see him after.

When I came back Brad and his girl were out in the street still discussing the wedding arrangements.

In fact, they were discussing them that passionately the cops were called.

I left them to it and went home happy to know an old mate and now a family man was moving in just down the road.

Then you're home one night and another mate rings up with one of those phone calls that are the last thing you want to hear.

Brad had gone out for a final fling on the Tuesday. His girl found him on the Thursday with the phone still in his hand. They were supposed to be married on the Saturday.

Brad's uncle, Leon, had died from a heart attack. His father had a triple bypass. Brad was 37.

What can you say? I suppose I could eulogise and steal other writers' quotes and say something like:

> The dead are like the stars by day,
> Withdrawn from mortal eye.
> But not extinct, they hold their way,
> In glory through the sky.

But I got a feeling Brad would tell me to get fair dinkum.

A few old sayings about Bondi people would be more appropriate.

'You can always tell a Bondi girl, but you can't tell her much.'

And: 'You can get the boy out of Bondi, but you can't get Bondi out of the boy.'

Well, they just took the boy out of Bondi and he'll be sadly missed.

I just hope the bloke upstairs likes a drink and a laugh. Because I've got a feeling it might start to get pretty giant up there from now on.

Especially when Bondi Brad and Fat Larry from Maroubra get together.

Aunty's ACES by me

A fellow writer buttonholed me in a pub the other day. She said her last book went okay, she'd finished another one and she'd done a marvellous interview for some literary segment on the ABC.

I replied good on her, she sounded like she was doing all right — better than me, in fact, because I never get interviewed on the ABC and I'm an awther of some repute.

To which she replied, that's understandable — after all the rotten things I'd said about the ABC, it was a wonder they didn't come around to my house at night, throw dead cats on my driveway and let my tyres down.

She was implying that I do nothing but bag them. When I drove home to the senile coast, I must admit I sat and pondered on this for a while.

Was I that rotten to Aunty? I don't really think so. For sure, I dumped on a couple of their so-called 'stars' who I thought were suffering badly from delusions of adequacy: like Trish Goddard and Tania Lacey.

And I did take the horsewhip to a bunch of old hens on 2JJJ who couldn't lay any more.

But not the ABC in general. For me to bag the ABC as a whole would not only be churlish and ignorant, it would be biting the hand that fed me.

I've done parts in movies on the ABC; always remembered my lines and greatly appreciated the work at the time.

The ABC makes great telemovies. Though when you're working on them you think they could build another Great Pyramid of Cheops in the same time, but they always turn out okay. *Scales Of Justice, Police Crop, Mail Order Bride, Lizard King,* just to name a few.

Which channel discovered *Minder*, the best show on TV? *Sesame Street, Beyond 2000, Dr Who* and *Yes Minister?* First-class viewing. If it wasn't for *Four Corners*, Bjelke and his cohorts would still be in power in Queensland.

Half those so-called stars getting absolutely ridiculous salaries started off on the ABC: Robbo, Carlton, etc. … Doug Mulray got his break on 2JJJ; the chosen one of course is in a class of his own supreme magnificence and eminence — Molly Meldrum, another Godhead created by the ABC …

Naturally, they have to flum a lemon now and again, like Jane Singleton. And all the dykes and the marxist feminists who can't get a bloke anyway have got a firm foothold in there, as have the horses' hoofs and the holier-than-thou, anti-racism bores who make it almost impossible to wear a white shirt these days without being called a racist.

Unfortunately, these tea-guzzling slugs have a penchant for burrowing their way into cushy little jobs in the public service — they're so entrenched you'd have had more chance of getting

Rudolf Hess out to Spandau than moving any of them.

However, that, along with the social security system, is just something we poor workers have to put up with.

And what channel gave us Selwyn Sprogget, arguably the greatest mind of our time? Time and time again I have prostrated myself towards Mecca and implored almighty Allah: Why doesn't the ABC repeat this show?

It's a gas. It was on in the late '70s, just about a miner in the north of England who rides his bike to the pub and says, 'Eeh, magic!'

You reckon you've come across some dumb Australians? This Pommie makes Terry McCann look like a rocket scientist.

But they won't repeat it. Which is typical of the ABC's racist, Pommie-bashing, discriminatory attitude towards humour from the north of England. The northist, humourist bastards!

But apart from that and Jane Singleton, Aunty's aces by me.

MADONNA: plenty to GRUMBLE about

The other day I picked up an old copy of *Playboy* and happened to flick to those nude photos of the beautiful Madonna, which caught my attention because I'd just read a couple of other things about her.

It was reported in some rag she looks like coming to Australia for a holiday — lucky us — and then I read an article in *People,* showing photos of her minders punching up some poor photographer for trying to snap her while she was jogging in Spain.

One big moron in particular was trying to lay the boot into the unfortunate photographer while he was on the deck.

So I got to thinking about Madonna and, to be quite honest, Madonna gives me the shits.

That's not to detract from the fact she's a multi-millionaire entertainer who sells millions of albums all round the world. She's an actress of sorts who's starred in big budget movies like *Dick Tracy, Desperately Seeking Susan,* etc.

Her fans flock to her concerts in their thousands and go for her records in the discos. But personally, I wouldn't cross the street to see her and, unlike that unfortunate photographer in Spain, there's no way I'd risk having some gorilla do a bit of Balmain folk-dancing up and down my rib cage for taking a photo of the peroxided scrubber.

I admit I might be a bit out-of-date with today's pop music and biased against Madonna from my days as a DJ working in various pits on the Central Coast, when I used to have to play 'Like A Virgin' and that atrociously boring 'Holiday' night after night. So what I dislike about Madonna might look like nothing more than my envy of the woman's well-deserved success. Not so.

Let's go back to those nude shots in *Playboy*. Anybody out there see them? They're in black and white, shot in a grotty flat full of cheap, daggy furniture.

Madonna herself looks about 20 — a whippy little body and nice firm tits.

But what about her minge? What do the Yanks call them? Beavers?

This is no beaver. This is more like one of those big, black bears you find running around in Alaska. I've seen a few teds in my day, but this is the daddy of them all. You could lose golf balls in it. Forget the map of Tasmania. We're talking Queensland rainforest here.

A Mujahideen warrior would give anything to have a beard as good as that. I reckon if you threw a newspaper in front of it, it would jump up and grab it.

If Madonna's going to do any sunbaking while she's in Australia, someone's going to have to explain the expression 'bikini-line' to her.

Then there are her armpits. They look like a couple of alpacas that drowned in sump oil. Possibly at the time Madonna was an earth mother or she might have been posing for an ad for Sunbeam razors or Makita weedeaters.

In future, if she's not worried about fixing her lamington, she could at least do something about her Warwicks. If not, buy a pair of overalls, move to Balmain and learn to play the bassoon.

If those necrophagous feminists on 2JJJ read this they're bound to accuse me of being sexist for talking about Madonna's crinoidal crumpet like this.

Madonna's a millionaire who poses for sexist photos. I'm sexist for talking about her bizzo, and the editor is sexist for publishing photos of it.

But by displaying this monstrosity isn't Madonna ultimately contributing to my sexism?

The other thing that pisses me off with Madonna is her new song, 'Justify My Love'. It's a dog of a song accompanied by a steamy video clip of several wallies having a bisexual group grope in a hotel room.

Yet here's Madonna being interviewed on TV as if she's some Nobel Prize-winning nuclear physicist: 'Y'know. This is my art. Y'know.'

Do they have to go on with all this bullshit just to flog some daggy pop record? What a dubbo. Give me Kate Ceberano any day. Still, you can't knock her for success and good luck to her. I'd like to swap bankbooks with her.

But can I make a suggestion? While she's in Australia she'll probably want to go jogging.

So to save her goons bashing up any more unfortunate photographers, why not take another photo of Madonna's grumble, untrimmed, absolutely *au naturel?* Then blow it up a bit bigger than poster size and have one of Madonna's gorillas hold it up with her jogging behind.

I don't know about anybody else — but if I saw that tarantula coming at me I'd run quicker than a goanna in front of a bushfire. It could have the street to itself. Adoration of Madonna maybe, but not that monster bearded clam. No way.

HOW to be AN AWTHER

Heaps of people write to me asking my advice about getting into writing. They send me little scripts and ideas etc. and I only wish I had the time to reply to all of them.

Unfortunately, there are just too many and it would cut too much into my drinking and drug-taking.

I also get other people, a little more belligerent, who approach me mainly in pubs. They look me up and down, poke their chests out and say, 'I'm gonna write a book too'. They really mean that if a mug like me can write a book, so can they, which is fair enough I suppose.

I wasn't bad at English at school but I'm definitely no Einstein.

I used to laugh at these people and they'd invariably get the shits. A couple of different sheilas even told me I was arrogant and conceited and to get myself well and truly %#@*!, which is also understandable I suppose.

They probably thought, like a lot of Australian authors, I was completely up myself. But I wasn't laughing at them, I was laughing at something else. So I changed my tack.

Now when they front me with their 'I'm gonna write a book', I just smile and say, 'Good on you. What are you going to do *then*?' That's the one that stuffs them. They just look at you and blink.

So I repeat the question. They end up just walking away. It's the perfect squelch.

The poor, silly bastards. They think you write a book, take it to some publisher, who welcomes you with open arms and says, 'Hi there. Thanks for bringing us your book. Here's $100,000 advance royalties. Let's do lunch.'

Hah! Are they in for a surprise! So for all those people who wrote to me about writing in Australia: I'm not trying to discourage you, but here are a couple of things you weren't expecting.

And believe your Uncle Bob: spending the best part of a year hunched over a typewriter, walking round the house talking to yourself, then staying awake half the night because you can't switch your mind off, and people thinking you're vague or more than likely half-mad while you're trying to get a novel together — that's the easy part.

It's when you've got it done and take it to a publisher … to use an old cliché … that, baby, is when the story really starts.

You'll more than likely meet some minion from the editorial department who'll look at you like you were something left over from a garbage strike.

After they've initially spat on you, set the dog on you and emptied the jerry over you for having the hide to bring the pile of shit in in the first place, they'll say, 'Leave it with us and we'll get back to you'.

About a month or so later they'll read the first six pages and the last four, then send you a letter politely telling you to stick it in your arse: 'Sorry, but we can't list it at the moment.' Ninety-nine out of 100 is the strike rate.

But say, you poor silly bastard, you're just that unlucky that they do accept it. You'll sign a memorandum of agreement, full of words and clauses that you don't understand till you find a couple of Arab oil sheiks on your doorstep come to take your sister away.

You might get $500 advance royalties and around 70 cents a book. But don't count on it. My first advance royalty was a counter lunch in a pub near Central Railway and I got 49 cents a book.

They'll print about 3000 that get a shelf life of three months. Meanwhile, you can piss off and they don't particularly care if they never see you again. Your book now goes to a cover designer.

Your novel might be about a stockman in the Snowy Mountains. Don't be surprised to find Bondi Beach and a Fijian holding a surfboard on the cover. While this is going on, your year's work is thrown to a creature called a sub-editor. It's hard to make a comparison to a sub-editor … drug squad coppers, parking police, heroin dealers?

I think they're more like fruit flies. They find a nice juicy peach, burrow into it and send the whole thing rotten.

They're either miserable feminists or frustrated academics with a low-mark PhD. They're flat-earthers totally removed from the real world and they're all frustrated writers.

They say inside every sub-editor there's a book dying to get out. And it's true. Only it's jammed in there like a big turd that no amount of epsom salts or herbal laxatives can shift.

In the meantime, seeing they can't write a book themselves, they'll make sure nobody else can. So they'll rehash your book to suit their miserable selves. You won't believe what they'll do to your stuff and, like they say in the army, there's not thing one you can do about it.

They've got the publisher behind them. He's hired the flips in the first place and has to justify the decision. And you're in there with your first book, convinced you're going to be the next Sidney Sheldon or Jackie Collins and you'll keep your mouth shut because you're not game to rock the boat.

I was always a little different. I could see I didn't have much to lose so I didn't only rock the boat — I used to torpedo it then machine-gun the lifeboats.

So your book sits out there and roughly two years after you rolled a sheet of A4 into your Olivetti you get your first royalties cheque. Probably for about $600 — out of which you deduct taxes, expenses, workers' compensation, sick pay, holiday and your 17.5 per cent loading.

But here's one you didn't think of. You're not writing waffle on an Arts Council grant; you're writing for the general public. So naturally the literary critics have to bag your book to show their superior taste and it lays an egg and sells about 200 copies. It's happened before.

And your royalties cheque, when it staggers in, is for $140. But your kindly publisher gave you a $500 advance, less $140 is $360. And that's what you owe your publisher. Pay up too, or they send the sheriff around.

I reckon it's beautiful. You spend over a year getting a book together and end up owing money. You'll find plenty of starving writers in Australia, but no starving publishers. I'm not trying to discourage you, but that's the way it is.

So if the next time you buttonhole me in a pub or whatever and tell me how you're 'gonna write a book', don't get the shits if I roar laughing.

I'm not laughing at you so much. What I'm really saying is, 'I'm glad it's you and not me'.

This isn't UNION BASHING but...

If it wasn't for the unions I wouldn't have my house, even if it is a dump.

In 1978 a hindquarter of beef fell on me when I was working in a meatworks in Sydney, knocking me flatter than a blob of cow shit.

I was on compo for a year before the insurance company cut out my payments. Three years later, through the union, I settled out of court.

I've still got a crook back and shoulders, and the amount I got wasn't all that much, but at least I didn't have to borrow all that much from the Shylocks at the bank. Just leave 20 litres of blood with my smiling bank manager and the rights to my corneas and all my internal organs if anything should happen to me.

So for me to indulge in even the most minute form of what could be termed 'union bashing' could possibly be construed as the act of a full-on unappreciative dropkick.

But no matter what you say about anybody these days — whether it's the police, public servants, schoolteachers — you're bashing them; it seems we've become so insular you're not even allowed a modicum of criticism.

But the unions have been in the news a bit lately so I thought I might pass comment. And might I say things have certainly changed in the union movement since I was a card-carrying socialist member of the AMIEU. Thank you comrades.

A garbage strike in Melbourne intrigued me. The aggrieved members stormed off the job because one of them got the punt for taking a sickie to go and work at another job.

That stinks like the garbage that piled up for more than a week till the union members reluctantly went back (plus the member who rorted the system and the ratepayers and left his fellow workers a man short while he earned a buck somewhere else).

It was a holiday weekend in WA so naturally the aircraft refuellers walked off the job. Somebody actually suggested they did a bit of work while they sat around on their fat arses waiting for planes to arrive.

Kicking and screaming and with faces longer than King Kong's wozzer, they went back to work.

And as soon as they did the refuellers in Sydney walked off in sympathy.

Stuff the poor mugs and families waiting for planes, the already half-stuffed tourist industry and fledgling companies like Compass trying to get going and maybe create a few jobs. Loafing, overpaid bludgers.

I don't know, I always thought if the job was that tortuous and the conditions so unbearable, if you had any balls you shot it in and got another one.

Remember I wrote about the public servant I knew who told me how big a bludge his job was — then went on strike not long after for more wages and better conditions?

The meatworks doesn't come within a bull's roar of the public service for a bludge, but we pulled the odd stroke now and again.

I was working at a shed in Sydney near Central Station; the worst part about it was that there was a pub next door. We were about to start work one morning and there weren't quite enough clean overalls to go round.

Out we stormed, up to the amenities room all po-faced for a meeting. We weren't going to cop this.

And the delo said: 'Okay. We all know the reason there are not enough overalls to go round is because we've been knocking them off. But that's beside the point.'

We lost half a morning's work and the pissheads went to the pub till the company bought more overalls, then we sulked our way back to work. The place eventually closed down and they all wondered why.

But the aggrieved members go out over the silliest things: sunglasses, the smell from a nearby Chinese restaurant, pie-warmers, even when they ran out of free beer at a Xmas party.

But take the dreaded sickie. Public servants scream at the merest suggestion of cutting back on their unlimited sick leave that we all pay for. But is there one worker in Australia who hasn't rorted a sickie?

I know I would have died before I'd take a sickie if I was genuinely crook. I'd rather go to work and suffer there.

Before I'd take a day off crook, I'd make sure I had eight hours' sleep and it was a perfect day and either go surfing or spearfishing. And if the waves or the fish were still on the next day, I'd have a relapse.

With people like Lang Hancock around, and that mob that run Robe River, you have to have workers' compensation, but I've seen it rorted. I used to be a big, bad Sydney wharfie; three months I lasted before I went off with the lockjaw from talking out the side of my mouth all the time.

I watched this gang carry a bloke in one morning who'd done his ankle playing touch football on the weekend. They got him halfway up the gangplank before he did the WWF's version of *Swan Lake*. It was truly a memorable performance.

They took him away moaning in agony on a stretcher and he went on compo. Good luck to him, I suppose, and it's good to have staunch mates. But it's a rort.

And the workers' compo act has definitely added to our multiculturalism. Besides spaghetti marinara our overseas friends have introduced 'Mediterranean back'.

And that grouse line that was going around: 'How do you tell the Greek in an Italian restaurant? He's the one with his neck in a brace.'

Wages are almost sacrosanct. Everyone is entitled to be paid what they're worth and what the boss can afford. But it's all the silly bloody conditions that are causing half the unemployment and a lot of the factories going to the wall.

But for conditions and perks you can't beat the public service. Take those fat cat pencil pushers in the ACOA. Besides making more money than they can possibly spend, they get leave loadings, higher duty allowances, study leave, maternity leave, compassionate leave, furniture and removal expenses, tea-stain allowance, paper-clip stress syndrome and, of course, the good old unlimited sickie. It runs into billions of dollars.

Besides nurses, ambos and coppers, i.e., public servants who actually earn their money, there's about another half-million out there.

If these public servants really tore their hearts out, suffered unbearable torture and self-sacrifice, and took just two fewer sick days a year — I know it's a lot to ask — but at around $100 a day, we taxpayers would save about $100 million.

How many jobs could the government create with that? How many pensioners could get a feed? How many street kids could be given a home and a bit of a chance?

Imagine if this spread through the workforce and we all stopped whingeing about conditions and we did a bit of work and got some extra money in our kicks, and if the boss makes a bit more, good on him or her.

We might even get on top of this recession and Australia might get back to where it was 20 years ago — a pretty good place.

Not a cross between the 51st State of America and a geisha house with Foster's on tap.

WHAT are you LAUGHIN' at?

How do you tell what's funny and what isn't? I don't ever class myself as a comedian like, say, Barry Humphries or Wendy Harmer — everything they write or say is supposed to be funny.

I think if you put your head up as a funnyman-person, it's a bit like laughing at your own jokes. I see myself more as a humourist.

I write this column for instance, about this-that-and-the-other and try to see the funny side of things. Some people get a laugh out of it now and again because they write in and tell me.

Others tell me to go shit in my hat. So I definitely don't see myself as a comedian. What strikes me as funny can be total anathema to somebody else. I've told jokes I thought were rip-snorters and they've gone over like a bomb in an air-raid shelter.

A critic in Melbourne even described my books as 'an extended version of the shaggy-dog story'. Which is fair enough, I suppose.

But I'm buggered if I know what's funny and what isn't.

A quote doesn't go astray, though. For instance, Peter Ustinov: 'Comedy is simply a funny way of being serious.' Or Lord Olivier: 'A comedian is closer to humanity than a tragedian. He learns not to take himself seriously.'

But one I like comes from Elsa Maxwell: 'Laugh at yourself first, before anyone else can.' It's hard to imagine a Yank saying that — in other words, get your head out of your arse and don't bore the tits off people.

So what makes me laugh, an alleged humourist and author of supposed shaggy-dog stories? One has to be careful here, because owning up to what you consider funny can tell a few home truths about you, and you might wish you'd kept your mouth shut.

I reckon Rodney Rude's funny. He's that ugly and obnoxious, how could he be anything else?

He reminds me of Mo McCackie on mescaline but he can tell a joke! I used to boo and hiss him at the Comedy Store in Sydney and would have given 10 years of my life to hit him in the face with a custard pie.

I couldn't get off on *The Big Gig*. It was a bit like the curate's egg, not bad in parts, but kept reminding me of that ABC 'aren't we oh-so-raunchy, different and clever' humour. Yet my darling grey-haired mother thought it was as funny as all get-up. And mother always knows best.

I still get a laugh out of those old Barry McKenzie movies. And has there ever been a greater insult to your sensitivities than Norman Gunston? He did for the in-depth TV interview what Pol Pot did for inner-city housing. Mike Gibson described him as 'the kid in class who always made awful smells'.

I'd swap 20 Steve Vizards and five Bryant Gumbels for him any day.

A good simile always turns me on. I think an all-time simile was the one by the Pommie journalist who described

Clive James as 'looking like a bank robber who forgot to take his stocking off'. You can't beat the Poms for humour on their day.

Was there ever a funnier show than *Fawlty Towers*? Oddly enough I did an ad with John Cleese and he's one of the most delightful people you'd ever care to meet, not at all like Basil.

Minder is a funny show, possibly my favourite, probably because as well as the cockney lingo, situations and characters, they weave a bit of pathos into it. Poor Terry, he no sooner gets it than Arthur takes it away.

Pathos to comedy is like garlic to a meal. A little can enhance the dish. Hello! That's not a bad author's quote for off the cuff.

I like fart jokes; which is why I gave that balding, stercoraceous gnome who does the breakfast show on 2MMM a rap. When it comes to a fart joke, Doug Mulray is the *capo di tutti capi*. Imagine being stuck in a mini-sub with him.

Irish jokes are starting to get a bit samey. And I'm not just saying that because my kinsfolk were some of the nicest people the English judges could send out here and the first bloke hanged in Australia was called Barrett.

Then there are all those 'didjahearabout' jokes. Like, 'did you hear about the wharfie who got killed when a forklift ran over his finger? He was picking his arse at the time.'

And of course the endless one-liners. 'I had a room in a hotel that was so dusty the mice walked round on stilts.'

'It was that long since they changed the bed, I had to get an electric jug and steam the sheets apart.'

'The publican's wife was that ugly that when they took the dog for a walk, people used to talk to the dog and pat her on the head.'

One-liners are punishing and they never end.

I can't get into those American sit-coms like *The Cosby Show*. This antiseptic story of some family of niggaz with affluence doesn't turn me on at all.

Yet one American show that completely cracks me up is *Barney Miller*. A bunch of cops in a New York precinct. It's multicultural humour that's drier than unbuttered toast. I'd rate it alongside *Minder*.

But being a bit bent, I like bent humour, and for bent humour it's hard to go past cartoonist Gary Larson, whoever and whatever he is. This is metaphysical humour from the fourth dimension.

I don't know anybody who doesn't like Larson. A lot of those American sheilas used to send me his cartoons and I know heaps of people with Larson desk calendars. I'd love to meet him.

However, now and again you find humour that truly inspires you. Writers need inspiration and if you're a writer-humourist you can't go past *Hustler* magazine for inspiration.

All flatophiles, sewerage works foremen and fat-and-bone truck drivers read *Hustler*.

Many's the time I've put on my old overcoat with the gravy stains and my dirty sandshoes and gone to the second-hand book shops at Central railway to buy old copies of *Hustler*.

It must be a good magazine; some redneck in the US shot the editor, Larry Flynt, whom he reckoned was the son of Satan. One *Hustler* cartoon sat on my office wall for five years.

Somehow I knew I had to write it into one of my books and I did, in the one that's coming out. I don't really know why, maybe it's just the way the dog is on the bed with its ears and eyes pinned back.

It reminds me of a dog I used to have. She was a grouse hollow log, a cross bull terrier-kelpie and I thought the world of the fat useless thing.

So shaggy-dog stories or whatever, I still can't tell you what's funny, but I just thought this was the least I could do for old Rosie.

Ayatollah of THE AIRWAVES

The editor of this illustrious magazine was talking about coming up and staying at my place for the weekend. He wanted to check out the sights and sounds of Terrigal.

The possums I feed had smashed all my plates bar one and I'd broken the spare cup so I was forced to drive over to a second-hand shop in The Entrance to get the said editor something to eat from and drink out of while he was here.

I had two bucks, but the cup and saucer only put me back 70 cents so I had over a dollar to spare and I found a pile of old records.

One was a ripper — *Chartstoppers. 20 Original Stars. 20 Original Hits.*

There were some top tracks on it. *Four in the Morning* — Faron Young. *Rock and Roll Lullaby* — B.J. Thomas. *Jesu Christo* — Kamahl. *Daddy Don't You Walk So Fast* — Daniel

Boone. And lo and behold — a track by John Laws: *A Front Row Seat To Hear Old Johnny Sing*. All this and more for only a dollar and, with John Laws on it, I knew it had to be good.

So with the cup, the plate, my grouse record and 30 cents left over, I headed home, where I drank half a bottle of bourbon, swallowed a bucket of prescription pills, boiled up a few angel's trumpets and got into it.

What a %*#@! of a %*#@! record. And that track by John Laws I was so keen to hear, it's one of those, 'Yeee-hah! Aah quit mah job and jumped a freight to Memphis' things. The kind of record you'd love if you had two heads, plucked a banjo and your kinsfolk didn't mind you trying to take your sister's cherry. It was horrible.

So I figure — if anybody, even John Bloody Laws, is game enough to go into a record studio and put down a catfish like that and rip a poor starving writer off for an oxford, I'm entitled to say my piece. I needed that dollar a lot more than John Laws does — that's for sure.

But what can you say about John Laws OBE? An Australian icon. Idol of thousands and probably the most powerful and influential man in radio, especially when you consider I quote pieces out of his column in Sydney's *Telegraph Mirror* to help prop up my own miserable effort.

Actually, I don't mind the 'mongrel' now and again. I'm not one of his blue-rinse Nazis who think the sun shines out of his skinny arse, but I listen on occasions — especially if he's got Hawke or some other top pollie in the studio. He talks sense — and that's a lot more than I can do at times.

He's national, so I imagine some *People* readers in other States have heard him.

The program starts with a monstrous drum-roll and a fanfare of trumpets that would leave the chariot race in *Ben Hur* for dead. Then there's the sound of a rocket ship hurtling through the galaxy to the strains of *El Presidenté*.

More fanfare and more sound effects. It's a cross between the coming of the Messiah and Cleopatra's entry into Rome. Then it's: 'Hello World. This is John Laws.'

With that intro who else could it be? Someone selling sandwiches? After the hosanna, it's straight into a plethora of ads followed by a plethora of jingles for the ayatollah of the airwaves.

'He's the voice. He's the king. He's Australia's number one. He's so far ahead he's lonely. He climbed Mt Everest backwards. He invented the radio-telescope. He was the first man on the moon etc. etc. ...'

Then the punters ring up. Along with their few brief moments to talk to the Messianic mystagogue they might get a rose, a bottle of Cloud Valley wine or a handful of John Laws' nuts.

They might also get told to piss off and don't ring back.

A likeable kid of about 12 rang up one day and Lawsie gave him a $5000 computer; just like that. For a grouch he can be a strange bloke.

When the chosen one makes a comment about something a thunderous voice booms in and says, 'Nobody says it like John Laws. Because there's only one John Laws.'

Then Lawsie says something else. In comes the voice: 'You've heard the rest, now hear the best. He's the voice of Australia. He's Mr Radio. Nobody but nobody can match John Laws.'

I reckon if Lawsie broke wind in the studio a voice would come booming in, 'You've heard farts — but nobody farts like John Laws.'

They go for it, though. Politicians would put their hands up their grandmothers' dress to get a few minutes on his show.

I couldn't class him as a greenie. He seems to be down on people that are for the environment and against woodchipping and other things.

And I can remember years ago when he had a late-night TV show. He was talking about some environmentalists who spent a few days and nights trying to save a pod of whales that had beached themselves somewhere.

Lawsie came on all sour-faced and said: 'Don't you think these people have gone just a bit too far this time?'

Bloody Hell! I hope he's changed his views since then. There are bugger all whales left and what there is the stinking Japanese are trying to harpoon into extinction.

Yet, paradoxically, he uses arguably Australia's best singer-songwriter and most popular greenie, John Williamson to do all his jingles. 'True Blue' should be Australia's national anthem.

He gets up the feminists and various ethnic whingers who love to have a go at him in court at the taxpayers' expense. The trouble is, he sails a bit too close to the truth for their comfort. His column is very good. Of course different ones in the media have to have a shot at him. He's a very tall poppy. It's sort of cool to bag a poor polio victim who's suddenly got 600 cars, 12 boats, five houses, money to burn and makes his own wine.

I reckon if you want to collect cars go for it — though I think after Dr Geoffrey Edelsten's last effort, personalised numberplates are a bit naff.

But Lawsie will have the last laugh. When he's sick of it all he'll retire to his farm, write his autobiography and it will be an automatic best-seller.

Though I can't say I envy his lifestyle. For all those who idolise him, there are an equal number who think he's the most loathsome reptile to ever crawl out of a tarpit.

He might have heaps of money but it's nice to be able to go places without some idiot having a shot at you, or being surrounded by sycophants trying to get a free plug on your show.

Money and power aren't everything. Lawsie likes to quote the *Bible* now and again and some of his kids have got biblical names. And what did Jesus say in the *Bible*? 'For what shall it profit a man if he shall gain the whole world and lose his own soul?' But good luck to Lawsie anyway. He's earned what he's got.

There is one thing I do envy about him. It's a 'covet thy neighbour's goods' type of thing. I'd give my left niagara to get my hands on his record collection.

Despite the thing I bought for a dollar, every now and again during his show Lawsie throws on some of the best rock'n'roll and country and western tracks I've ever heard. For talkback radio, the music's pretty good.

I reckon he would have one of the best record collections in Australia. He'd have stuff from all over the world, stuff you've never heard of. Imagine getting amongst it!

I wonder if I sent him a book and wrote to him saying: 'Dear Mr Laws, I am a poor starving writer living on the Central Coast not far from you. I listen to your show, I've got all your records and I dig your poetry. Any chance of coming around to Cloud Valley and taping a few tracks?'

I wonder how I'd go? No, I reckon knowing my luck, I'd get told to piss off and don't call back. The most I could expect would be a handful of John Laws' mouldy old nuts.

Still, after looking at that Pickering calendar, it couldn't be any worse than a front-row seat to hear old Johnny sing.

Starstruck? Not us SCORPIOS

I imagine there aren't too many readers out there who at some time in their life haven't bothered to consult their horoscope in a paper or magazine and taken, if nothing else, a token interest in their star sign.

Which doesn't mean you have to be like some poor wallies who won't leave their house unless the moon is up Uranus or Mickey Mouse is into Pluto. That's ridic.

But I take an interested observer's view of the zodiac. I glance at my horoscope in the morning paper and quite often it can have an uncanny coincidence.

Like it might say, 'a pressing source affecting your work and a family relationship will emerge this week'. True. Various cheques from various publishers don't arrive and I don't get to eat.

Then dear mother will ring and give me a blast over the phone. It's about time I settled down, woke up to myself, stop being such a dill, you're just like you father, where's the money you owe me, bleah, bleah.

I tell you, it's a bummer when the doctor won't give the old girl any more tranquillisers.

Other times your horoscope might say, 'things are unstable now because of the full moon'. This can also turn out to be true.

Once I OD'd on angel's trumpets again and thought I was a werewolf. I was howling away on the deck and the railing gave way and I nearly broke my back.

I was going all right too, because I live in the Harlem of Terrigal and no-one around here can afford a silver bullet. They threw plenty of half-empty beer cans, plastic bags of dog shit and plonk bottles, but it takes more than that to stop the Bela Lugosi of the Central Coast when he gets a roll on during a full moon.

But as much as I believe there could be something in people's star signs or the zodiac, what you read in your daily horoscope is as much coincidence and theory as anything else. And I'll drop a real good name here to prove my point.

A Russian scientist. Aleksander Isaacovich Kitaigorodski. He said: 'A first-rate theory predicts, a second-rate theory forbids, a third-rate theory explains after the event'. So your horoscope is basically a third-rate theory with a bit of 20/20 vision in hindsight thrown in.

If anyone is remotely interested, I'm a Scorpio. The swingingest, sexiest, most wonderful sign in the zodiac. Vindictive, spiteful, sarcastic, able to leap tall buildings and bear grudges for a lifetime. Then, on the other hand, I'm supposed to appreciate a good laugh and repay favours with almost astounding generosity.

I like to think we're the ones with the third eye. Talking with other Scorpios, we seem to see things in people others can't; unless you're a Scorpio though, you wouldn't understand. And haven't there been some good Scorpios?

Charles Manson, Terry 'Mr Asia' Clarke, Harry M. Miller, John Singleton. A lot of top generals were Scorpios: Rommel, Montgomery, Patton and Colonel David Hackworth, the most decorated living soldier in US military history. He mentions this in his book I keep telling people to read, *About Face*.

Picasso and Richard Burton weren't bad blokes though.

And talk about Scorpio generosity. The late Richard Burton must have thought Liz Taylor pretty good in the porking department — he bought her a $5 million diamond ring.

So how do I, a sarcastic Scorpio and possessor of the third eye, find other members of the zodiac without coming across as a zodicist? Do they have similarities?

I seem to get on good with Aquarians. I've been involved with a number of Aquarian women and almost married two. I find them sexy, with this zany, nonchalant sense of humour.

Then you have Ronald Reagan and Joh Bjelke. You can't possibly tell me all their scones were done.

As far as porking goes, the wildest, most uninhibited girl — again — I almost married was a Virgo. Initially, yes. But in the end it was anything goes, no holds barred, anytime, anyplace, anywhere. It was almost too much for a poor, young surfie to handle.

Geminis are said to have split personalities. I took one out for a while. A nice enough girl sober, but four Bacardis and Coke and she'd start a fight in an empty house.

Scorpios are said to be the sexy sign of the zodiac and I admit I don't mind a bit of the other. I'm quite partial. I also never got a knockback from my sweet ladyfriends. If anything it was the other way around.

I often laugh when I see different women's groups marching around with signs saying 'Regain the Night'. When I'd come home from the meatworks after boning 100 forequarters and

100 briskets since 5.30 a.m., they could regain the bloody night, they could regain the rest of the week for all I cared. I couldn't lift a nightie.

Despite their alleged sexiness, I've always tried to steer clear of affairs with fellow Scorpios. Not out of discrimination or sexual aversion. But say the lady involved became pregnant. Wouldn't the child involved be an inbred?

So you're a sexy Scorpio checking out other Scorpios to see if they have any similarities. My birthday is November 14, and who should have his on the same day? None other than HRH Prince Charles, the future King of England.

And blow me down if there aren't some striking similarities. We've both got big noses, our ears stick out and we're both going bald on top. Plus, I read, he likes salami and talks to himself. How about that?

But there it seems to end. Chilla's the man who's supposed to be into conservation and his father, Phil the Greek, is a member of some world wildlife preservation foundation. There wouldn't be two more trigger-happy Hooray Henrys on the planet.

They like nothing better than to get out on the royal estate armed to the teeth and blast anything that moves with shotguns. They make the NSW duck season look like a Buddhist picnic.

It runs in the whole silly bloody family. Edward VIII had his old man's dogs shot because one of them pissed on his leg.

When Edward was the Prince of Wales, they came back empty-handed after a day's shooting and saw this beautiful little deer grazing by the castle. So they blew it to bits. It turned out to be a gift from the people of Alberta, Canada — a symbol of friendship.

Another royal went hunting, couldn't find a deer in the fog-shrouded hills so he shot one of the royal ponies.

They still do it. As good a reason as any to get rid of the monarchy, I suppose.

But no. I'll stick my neck out and say we should retain the monarchy and I'll fight tooth and nail before I see them change the flag and turn Australia, land that I love, into a republic.

Not so much out of love for the royal family … but if another one of Queen Elizabeth's corgis bites her and she dies of rabies and the IRA doesn't blow Charlie to bits and the gun-crazy, big-eared git makes it to the throne, it'll be a public holiday on my birthday.

Which means I can get blind, rotten, shit-your-pants, vomiting drunk and not go to work and no-one can say a word. Could an Australian ask for anything more?

MAD WAX before Thunderdome

There was an item in the paper the other day: film producer George Miller, of Kennedy-Miller fame, was said to be the man who discovered Mel Gibson.

Miller cast him in the first *Mad Max* movie, then the other two which became box office hits, making Gibson an international superstar.

'He had that something about him,' Miller is alleged to have said. I took umbrage and offence at this. I also felt like taking a few palings and the front door as well.

Why? Because I have a world exclusive on the man who discovered Gibson, took him under his wing and launched him on his rise to stardom.

I should know, because I was offered the part of Gibson's stand-in in his first movie. And you better believe it.

As far as actors go I don't mind Gibson, especially when he gets that nutty look in his eyes and his head kind of oscillates.

I haven't seen his latest movie *Omelette;* I just can't picture poultry farms in Shakespeare's day. But I enjoyed *Lethal Weapon* and its sequel, and I liked all the *Mad Max* films.

Though I can't say I went overboard about *The Bounty*. But the one movie of Gibson's that I really dug was that Australian classic *Summer City*. It was produced and scripted by the man who *did* discover Mel Gibson — Phil Avalon.

He's the unsung hero of Australian films who, in my professional opinion, produces movies that make anything Kennedy-Miller or Fred Schepisi come up with look like Jackie McDonald's *Home Video Show*.

I was sharing a flat at Tamarama in the early '70s. Phil lived just across the road. He'd been down from Newcastle for a year or two, drove a sports car, did parts in TV commercials and appeared to be getting things together in the film industry. Phil's flat was right on the beach and there was always a bevy of glamours hanging around outside — of which Phil married one. I went to his parties, he came to ours, we rode lids and skis and over the years Phil and I became pretty good mates.

I even let him talk me into buying a surfski off him.

Phil made Wavemaster skis and as well as being a hot salesman, he's a hot ski rider too. But back to the swinging '70s.

I arrived home from the pickle factory one afternoon and noticed Phil and this film crew zooming around Tamarama and Bronte in a black '63 Chevy with a stack of nine-foot mals on the roof. Naturally I inquired what was going on.

Phil was shooting a movie. An action drama with a surfing theme, set in the '60s. I was impressed. We all were. Hollywood had come to Tamarama. The boy from Newcastle had come good.

I watched the carryings-on over the weeks and one afternoon Phil walked up to me and said, 'Hey, Barrett. You can ride a surfboard all right?' I nodded yes because then I could. 'How would you like to come up to Catherine Hill Bay and be a stand-in for this actor in my movie?'

'Who is he?' I asked.

'Mel Gibson. I just got him and another actor, Steve Bisley, straight out of NIDA. It's their first gig.'

'And this Gibson bloke can't surf?'

'Mate, he couldn't wax a surfboard, let alone ride one. But he's a hot actor and he's got this something.'

I knew from inside sources that Phil's movie was not only being shot on a shoestring, the budget was that skinny it could walk through a harp.

For me to take three days off from the pickle factory, plus petrol and expenses, it would probably cost me more than it would be worth. Still, there would have to be some sort of an earn there, and it could be fun. I thanked Phil and said I'd be in it for sure.

The following afternoon I was watching the filming. They wrapped, then the director, producer, actors and crew went into a huddle. There'd been an unexpected budget blowout and they didn't have enough petrol to get to Catherine Hill Bay.

The huddle continued then Phil handed Gibson a length of hose and a plastic jerry-can and told him to go and milk a tank of gas from a car that had rolled over a cliff at Tamarama. And if Bisley wasn't doing anything, he could give him a hand.

I figured if this was how Phil treated the leads, the stand-in's earn would be very frugal indeed. Some bread and treacle, an IOU and he'd probably want to use my EH ute in a running gun battle. I thanked Phil all the same, but told him I couldn't get the time off work.

While I was boning rumps and loins in Sydney, they got to Catherine Hill Bay. Ross Bailey, a.k.a. 'The Nail', doubled for Gibson in the surfing sequences. The whole thing fell into place.

The only mild blemish was when Bisley and Gibson decided to moon the Catholics having a full-on wedding at the local community hall.

If only the congregation and the blushing bride had known that the hairy white date going past in the window of the black '63 Chevy belonged to Mel Gibson, they'd have been even more impressed.

Summer City premiered and we all went to see it, and it didn't turn out half a bad flick either, becoming a cult film.

It's got a punchy rock'n'roll soundtrack and the surfing scenes shot in Catherine Hill Bay almost 20 years ago, that I knocked back, are now classics. It's definitely not *Gone With The Wind* and it never made the Cannes Film Festival, but what do you expect for $60,000? Yep, that's how much it cost to make.

These days it would cost that just to keep Cher's hairdresser on the set.

Gibson went on to become one of the highest-paid film stars in the world, Bisley is an accomplished actor who starred in one of Australia's biggest grossing movies, *The Big Steal*.

The biggest rub is that *Summer City* is still selling all over the world. From Senegal to Saskatchewan, Los Angeles to London, people walk into video stores and see this Australian surfing drama with Gibson in it and think, 'Hey! This'll be all right'.

Phil's still making movies, he's now got a lovely family and lives in a beautiful house right on Narrabeen beach where he spends most of his time surfing one of the best breaks in Australia outside his back door.

He probably thinks back on all those smartarse remarks we made when he was shooting that movie in Tamarama and more than likely loves them. It gives him something to laugh about when he's walking down to the bank.

Phil is about to start shooting another movie near Noosa Heads with Linda Blair of *The Exorcist* fame called *Fatal Bond*. I pulled the old mate's act out the other day and rang him to see if there was something there for me. I can run half-a-dozen words together when I need to.

Unfortunately no, Phil said, but he did say to ring a mate at Channel 10. They could use my head on *Neighbours*. Somebody knocked off their door-stop.

He's not a bad bloke, is our Phil.

Oddly enough, he's giving another Gibson his first gig in this movie — Donal Gibson.

That's right. Mel's little brother. I don't know if he can act let alone whether he's got 'that something'.

But having knocked around with Phil Avalon, I just hope he knows what to do when the producer hands him a length of hose and an empty jerry-can. After all, it's a lot further from Sydney to Noosa than it is to Catherine Hill Bay.

Say your PRAYERS VARMINTS!

Once again the duck season is well and truly under way.

I've already said my piece on the duck season and got letters from duck hunters wanting to fill my arse with buckshot for my trouble — so I won't dwell on a boring and distasteful subject.

Though I will say some of the hunters seemed to have brushed up their act a little this year. A few of those who just want to go and get a feed admit there is a majority of imbeciles running around full of piss shooting anything that moves.

Some others have admitted all that lead going into the wetlands is doing for the ecosystem what the RAF did for the highway system in Iraq, so I don't think it would be too much to ask the munitions factories to change from leadshot to something less damaging to the environment.

I still reckon duck shooting with shotguns is about as much a sport as killing baby harp seals used to be.

And any of those hunters or spokesmen for the gun lobby who say it's a quick and painless death ... I'll make you a deal. Fly over the wetlands in a hang-glider and let me blast you with a few rounds of 12 gauge and if it doesn't hurt I'll give you $1000.

I'll also stick by my word and say that shotguns are a disgraceful and inhumane weapon and should be banned, even from the police, especially the TRG. Look what they did to that unfortunate Darren Brennan.

And in Sydney, a hard-working family of panel beaters were just going about their business and two creeps ran in armed with shotguns demanding money. The people had none at the time so as they left, the heroes let go a couple of shots. They didn't kill anybody, but they managed to blind one of the family. Fun things, shotguns — aren't they?

However, despite being a member of Greenpeace and a lover of birds and animals, I'm not one of those beansprout-eating, lefty peaceniks who are down on anything remotely to do with violence or a drop or two of blood.

There's nothing wrong with guns. Guns are good. Guns are fun. Like the gun lobby says, guns don't kill people, people kill people.

Of course, if people didn't have any guns they wouldn't be able to kill and if someone came at me with a gun or a knife I know what I'd take my chances against. The bottom line is, guns are deadly and they kill. They don't make them to pour cappuccinos.

But there are thousands of them out there, bought, registered and paid for by citizens who have a right to use them — sports shooters.

These people are entitled to go out into the countryside, enjoy the trees and serenity of nature and kill something. And if they're not drunken weekend Rambos shooting anything that moves it's quite all right.

And what's the biggest problem facing farmers at the moment, besides banks, feral pigs and the stuffed wool and wheat yields? Another species introduced by our forebears — rabbits.

Evil, skulking, insidious, wife-stealing, backstabbing rabbits. These cute, cuddly little bastards are stuffing up the countryside at the rate of knots.

The cockies have poisoned them, dynamited them, bayoneted them and they still don't know how many there are. Two hundred million was one count. That's in NSW.

Actually, it's no bloody joke. Ask any farmer. The bastards will devastate a hectare of prime grazing land in 48 hours. They're %&$@! of things. Forget the *Bible* and Pontius Pilate. It was the Easter Bunny that shelved Jesus Christ. But how do we get rid of the floppy-eared, cotton-tailed little dropkicks?

I reckon the NSW Government should legalise machine-guns. Now immediately those tofu-eating, pinko bleeding hearts will start jumping up and down saying we can't have people running around with submachine-guns.

I'm not talking about Uzis, or AK–47s or Heckler and Koch MP5A2s. I'm talking .22 submachine-guns. Nothing more than a souped-up pea rifle. Over 50m they'd be flat out wounding, let alone killing, a human being.

But if 10,000 sports shooters had these .22s, not just fully automatic but rock'n'roll, the little grey bastards wouldn't know what hit them. If those sports shooters didn't eliminate the rabbit population in a year I reckon they'd about halve it.

I've thought of this sensational idea from all angles and I can't see what's to stop it. The guns would be licensed and accounted for in the proper manner from which the State Government and the police would make a nice profit.

Ecologically there are no problems. Don't use lead. The CIA and Mossad have bullets made from various alloys which are environmentally friendly and look like mini-grenades going off when they hit you.

The farmers would be as happy as Larry because you'd be getting rid of the rabbits and, at the moment, our farmers need all the help they can get.

'Ah, pigs,' I hear someone say. Yes, feral pigs too, another introduced species which is also stuffing up the environment. Purists will say a .22 won't stop a feral pig. One shot won't, maybe.

But I don't care if it's the biggest, meanest #@*% of a pig in Australia. If he comes charging at me with his tusks flailing and three seconds later he's got 10 bullets in his head, that would have to slow the bludger up considerably.

A few more shots would blow their heads to the wastelands of Krolnor where they would be eaten by the Scalebs.

As for messing up the landscape — pick out the best bits of rabbit, to be baked slowly with rosemary and white wine and basted with garlic butter. Exceedingly scrumptious. The rest, just dig a hole and toss it in with a few seeds or a sapling. Where once there were rabbits there would then be beautiful forests, all naturally fertilised.

Controlled by the police and the government, we'd have the biggest rabbit cull ever and everybody gets an earn — from the farmers to the munitions factories right along to the tourist trade.

Fly in all those gun crazy Seppos and boxheads, give 'em a .22 and 1000 rounds and let 'em go for their lives. They'd love it.

Is this idea any more stupid or heartbreaking than having to watch our farmers shoot their sheep? I can't see an argument from anybody on this idea — from the greenies, through the government to the gun lobby.

It has to be better than a team of drunks running around with shotguns shooting swans and kookaburras.

And those sweet little bunnies with their cute little noses and cute little paws? They'd get, 'Nyeh! What's up doc?' right up the khyber. From around 10,000 shooters. Anyway you like it baby. Fully automatic or rock'n'roll.

AMBOS have to COP IT SWEET

Okay, so I bag public servants every now and again, ones from the ABC and pen-pushers in government departments, on a terrific rort and still whingeing.

This doesn't mean I'm crooked on public servants in general.

Do I ever bag customs officers, or people who work for the national parks and wildlife? They're public servants.

And if I ever say anything bad about nurses you can break my typewriter over my big boofhead.

I more or less got confronted by a number of public servants the other day who recognised me through *People*.

They took me to task over some of my remarks about government workers, namely ambulance officers — 'ambos'.

I bumped into them in a hotel in Sydney having a farewell drink for one who was retiring after 20 years on the job. There were about 12 of them, men and women. They lived and worked between Sydney and Newcastle.

So what do I know about ambos?

They revive junkies who have OD'd and they pull people out of wrecked cars. They go through a fair bit of trauma and see ghastly, horrible things that we, the general public, never see.

That's about it.

Hah! That's the easy part. These hard-working men and women are being driven mad by bureaucrats and imbecilic loafers, bludging their way through life on social security.

They witness rorts that cost taxpayers millions and put up with some of the greatest dills imaginable.

And the other good thing is, they can't say a word about it or they get disciplined and possibly lose their job. It's unreal. I'll give you some examples.

Doctors make appointments for ambulances to take people to their surgeries or to see specialists — they're too lazy to get off their arses and catch a taxi or get on a bus or train. Half the time there's bugger-all wrong with them.

On the way back from the specialist or doctor these 'cripples' will put it on the ambos to wait while they go and do their shopping.

They'll get called out to a housing commission home where a woman's about to have a baby. They arrive to find three cars in the driveway. If they ask why couldn't the family take her to the hospital, the woman will say: 'Me 'usband's asleep, me son's gone round to 'is girlfriend's house and me daughter's got to go to the 'airdresser.'

They'll get a call, 'man with lacerated hand' or 'woman with severe abdominal pains'.

Lacerated hand turns out to be some egg with a scratch on his finger that barely needs a Band-aid. When they ask why they couldn't fix it themselves, it's: 'I didn't have no Band-aids. But don't worry mate, I'm on social security.'

Severe abdominal pains turns out to be an 18-stone drunken heap of a sheila who's come home from the RSL convinced she's got food poisoning. So mum rings an ambulance.

The ambos arrive just as a little head pops out and mother who called the ambulance is now a granny.

They're that stupid they didn't even know she was pregnant. But it's okay, they're on social security.

These pensioners and the like are convinced they have a God-given right for an ambulance to be at their disposal 24 hours a day.

People in minor car accidents with not a scratch on them and the ambos have to more or less con them into signing a 'refuse transport' form so they can get to some bloke bleeding to death in an industrial accident.

The ambos can't refuse anybody, even when it's blatantly clear there's not a thing wrong with them.

And if they so much as say a word or finally blow up and tell some bludger to wake up, they'll get a complaint against them and have to front their superior for disciplinary action.

The superior, I might add, is a dead-set public servant who should spend time out in the trenches with the troops.

These dedicated men and women are being stuffed around by bludgers who get everything given to them on a plate. It's the ambos vs the imbos.

Of course, the job does have its droll moments. Like the time a call for severe burns turns out to be a smoker sitting on the pan in his outhouse. The pan had just been emptied and the dill forgot he'd washed it out with kero. After he'd finished having a dump and reading the paper, he dropped his cigarette butt in the pan and almost blew his nuts off.

You want burns? I'll give you burns. A truck overturns just past Newcastle and bursts into flames. An off-duty cop pulls the driver out — he's got third-degree burns.

When the ambos arrive the driver's not in any pain because all his nerve endings are seared away.

He says, 'I feel like a barbecued sausage'. He looks it too.

He's got about an hour to go. There's nothing the ambos can do but talk to him and tell him he's gonna be okay.

If he's lucky he'll get a doctor who'll just OD him on morphine. That's before they cut him open so all the gasses and body fluids can run out and he doesn't literally explode when everything inside him shuts down from the severity of his burns.

They get called to a house where grown-ups were having a bit of a party and now the ambos have to try to resuscitate three two-year-olds who have drowned in the pool. But it's too late. They can live with it, but they're not allowed to talk about it.

Pulling injured people and mutilated corpses out of cars. How about crawling in and getting them out from underneath trains? If they're not under the wheels they're spread about half a kilometre along the track.

People think ambos live for the buzz of screaming down the road, sirens wailing, lights flashing, forcing cars to the side of the road. Then when they arrive, after risking their lives and those of other drivers on the road, they find some bum on social security who needs a Band-aid on his finger.

It's not that long ago that they didn't have two in an ambulance and one person had to do all the work. And even now, when they get back to the station they can't ring home to see if the kids got home from school all right or to say they're okay or they might be home late because the government won't put a phone in the station. Not even a blue payphone which costs a lousy $200.

Yet various ministers, whom we won't name, don't mind spending millions on consultants, on doing up their offices or on flying around the world. Isn't saving just one life worth $200?

Despite the ambos not being able to tell me anything I did manage to earwig a few things while I was with them in the pub, and the bloke from Newcastle who was retiring didn't really give a stuff because he was getting out anyway.

Among other things, he told me of a sure-fire cure to the heroin and junkie problem. Unfortunately, it's too practical and I can't repeat it here. Plus it might upset a few bleeding hearts.

But he did tell me a bit of a story about doctors he didn't like. Not your friendly local GP, but smartarse interns in hospitals, just out of uni, all bright-eyed and bushy-tailed and full of their own importance.

The veteran ambo had pulled a body out of a car smash and took it to hospital. He went in and told the intern he had a body in the ambulance, could he get it out of the road.

The budding Dr Kildare tapped the ambo with his stethoscope and said, 'I'm the doctor here. I'm the one who signs the certificate and says whether they're dead. Not you. Okay?'

It wasn't a bad show in front of the nurses so the veteran ambo copped it sweet. He just wanted to get back to saving lives. He just didn't have time for all the bullshit.

A week or two later he pulls two more bodies out of a car wreck, goes to the same hospital where the same doctor is on duty and says the same thing to him. The ambo would by this time know if someone was dead or not.

But again he gets, 'Didn't I tell you before I'm the doctor, not you? I'll say whether they're dead or not. Can you get that into your head?'

Not being able to say anything the ambo again cops it sweet. Not long after that, he gets called to an industrial accident.

A decapitation. A worker got hit in the neck by a slab of steel which took his head clean off.

The veteran ambo took the body to the hospital knowing the same intern was on duty. When he got there though, he took the head out of the plastic bag and placed it on the corpse's feet.

Then he walked inside and very politely said to the doctor, 'Excuse me, I've got a bloke out here who's been pretty badly hurt in an accident, but I'm not sure if he's dead or not. Do you think you could come and have a look?'

I thought I'd leave the column there because not long after that I left the ambos to their partying. Besides, it was his day, the old bloke who was retiring. They didn't want me around hearing things I'm not supposed to.

RACIST yes, SEXIST fine, TOBACCONIST NO!

One thing I try my best to avoid is repeating myself. However, if it's more than a year since you've written about something, I don't see why you can't reiterate the subject without boring the tits off your readers.

I've already done a column on cigarettes, but they've been bobbing up in the news more and more lately. I'll stick by what I previously said about cigarettes.

They stink and I reckon anybody who smokes has got rocks in his or her head. But this column isn't necessarily another diatribe against smokers. Even though they can be a pain in the arse, I feel a little sorry for them. They're being ripped off by both the government and the cigarette manufacturers in what I consider is a nice little conspiracy. A definite collusion between the two.

So this time I'm not completely ripping into the poor, silly smokers.

This is about tobacco.

Different things have brought cigarettes to my attention lately — apart from seeing butts squashed out everywhere you walk and ash all over the tickets in the TAB.

Los Angeles State Prison was one. You should see this place — it was built to hold 15,000 inmates and is holding 22,000, mainly blacks and Hispanics.

In July it's going smoke-free and as most of the cons smoke, they're expecting riots.

This could prove interesting watching. Thousands of horrible cons going through nicotine withdrawal. There's nothing like a good riot on the TV news and the Yanks pull off some rippers.

My publisher now has a smoke-free building. You can actually walk through the dungeons there without squinting all the time. Airlines are starting to go smoke-free. All you need at altitude is for some dillberry to drop a cigarette butt in a bin full of paper towels. It's not as easy as it used to be for the smokers to walk around dragging on a dotch. Though you can still ruin your health and your clothes till all hours in discos and bars. But soon some barperson will put in a claim for a work-related sickness and that'll finish that.

The thing that caught my eye though, was the book *Modern Merchants Of Death* by Tim Hewat. Tim is an ex-60-Gitanes-a-day man hired by the cigarette companies to do some spying for them. Instead of spying, Tim did a big dump.

He writes: 'It makes one focus a good deal more sharply on what smoking is all about, on what a killer on a mass scale it really is, and how outrageous are the benign attitudes to the slaughterous trade adopted by the transnational tobacco companies.'

Tim's book doesn't quite parallel the conspiracy I'm coming to. But being an ex-smoker like Tim, I have an empathy towards smokers and how they're being discriminated against. Uncle Bob understands. You just gotta have that dotch. Not every now and again. About every five #$@&* minutes.

To expect you to clean up your shit after you and not blow or let smoke drift in non-smokers' faces is a big ask. Smokers have got rights. Rights to stuff up their own health and everybody else's too.

The best thing about cigarettes though, is all the crap they're wrapped in. There's saltpetre, nitric something or other, and about 20 other poisons the cigarette companies put in the low rotten things to make them burn.

Still, like I said, smokers have got rights, they pay heaps in taxes and still manage to make millions for the tobacco companies.

But what is a cigarette smoker? He's nothing more than a drug addict — addicted to nicotine, and in a bad way. Some are worse than others. Same as smackies gotta have a hit of heroin, cokeheads gotta have a line, mullheads like a cone, crankheads gotta do some speed ... smokers just gotta have a dotch.

The young idiots think it's image. They're just trainee addicts. After 10 years of forking out around $30 a week to give yourself lung cancer, *then* you're an addict. And all addicts need help. Yet all nicotine addicts can do for their habit is to buy increasingly expensive packets or cartons of cigarettes.

Why shouldn't chronic nicotine addicts be allowed to grow their own tobacco? Just a nice little plant where they can fill a pipe or make a roll-your-own, enough to ease the craving.

There'd be less pollution, no butts all over the place and the poor nicotine addicts would save a fortune. Plus, they wouldn't be sucking in all that poison from the chemically-treated papers and tobacco the cigarette companies sell.

This is where smokers are being discriminated against.

It is discrimination too. If you're an alcoholic you get counselling. If you're coming off coke you get that plus medication. If you're a low-life heroin addict robbing old ladies or hawking your fork and spreading AIDS, they'll give you methadone and put you on a pension.

Yet the poor old smokers get zilch.

The smoker is being bled dry by the capitalist vampires running the tobacco industry and being discriminated against by the government. And if there's one thing I hate it's discrimination. I might be racist and a sexist, but I'm not a tobacconist. It stinks.

It's a collusion forged between the tobacco companies and the government because the tobacco companies are terrified they'll lose money.

Look at it this way and tell me it's not a rort. I can grow my own vegetables. Does this send the farming industry broke? My mother's been making her own jam for years. Did this cause a crisis at SPC?

If I live in the bush I can have my own eggs and eat the chickens. Have my own milk and, if I want to, slaughter the cow and fill the freezer full of meat. I can have sheep and knit my own jumpers. Does this make the wool industry any worse off?

I can brew my own piss, make it as strong as I want, the type I want and share a bit around. Are home brewers sending the breweries broke?

I can't distil my own spirits, but that's mainly because of health and safety regulations. Though I've worked with plenty of migrants who get a little co-op going and make their own wine. Especially these Portuguese blokes I worked with once. I don't know of any wineries going to the wall.

You can't manufacture your own heroin or cocaine but I reckon if the government ever works out a way of making money from the mullheads it'll soon be legal to grow your own pot.

But the poor bloody cigarette smoker gets shafted by both the tobacco companies and the government and turned into an addict at the same time. Yet if you get caught trying to grow tobacco, even to help your addiction, it's an unbelievable pinch.

Something like a $6,000 fine and three years gaol. Why such a heavy pinch? It's only a plant and it's not an illegal substance.

You don't have to read Tim Hewat's book to know why. I wouldn't mind acting the bush lawyer here and wondering if some smartarse barrister put this to both the tobacco companies and the government what the answer would be?

There's collusion there and there's definitely some sort of a case for conspiracy. And there's no way it's not discriminatory, against people addicted to nicotine, the good old smokers.

Whatever the end wash-up, I couldn't give a stuff about cigarettes. I don't like the mess, the smell, what it does to my clothes or health.

But smokers are getting a hard time at present, apart from the expense. There are more restrictions all the time, it's getting harder and harder to dotch around other people and it will only get worse.

Non-smokers are starting to win the battle. Consequently the tobacco companies are spending a fortune on lawyers and advertising defending smokers' rights. Which they should, they can certainly afford it.

Personally, I don't deny anybody the right to smoke. But I am curious as to why the tobacco companies won't allow smokers the right to grow their own.

A Tour DE BONDI

For months now I've been promising myself a 10-speed bike. I've had one and they're great. My present model, however, is in the backyard, rusting away with weeds and vines growing through it. It's a photographer's delight.

I ended up getting another one — flat tyres, rusty with a ton of junk all over it. I don't know what it was worth but it ended up costing me about $1000.

After nine years up here on the beautiful Central Coast, scrimping, saving and being arrested and gaoled, I decided I needed a break.

I was two books in front and, apart from the constant pressure of writing this column, I didn't have all that much to do and I actually had a little bit of money in the bank.

But, after sitting around picking my toes for a while, the writing bug bit me and I knew I had to do something. I needed new fields to conquer. So I thought I'd have a go at writing a play. There's an earn in it if you're successful, plus the prestige of being a playwrite as well as an awther and I figured after writing a 300-page book, penning 100 pages of waffle and dialogue would be as easy as pissing the bed when you're drunk.

I've got a book of Neil Simon's plays, which I perused and came up with a plot — stealing a few of Simon's ideas. Never be afraid to steal other writers' lines and ideas. There are plenty out there nicking mine, besides, imitation is the greatest form of flattery.

The only problem with my play was instead of being in New York it was set in Sydney, and to get this wobbegong together would mean moving down there for research. I couldn't afford to rent a flat and I'd be flat out staying at the People's Palace let alone the Sebel Town House while I got it together.

So I went for the old 'share accommodation' rort. There must be people out there who have done it. I have, heaps of times in the past and you know what to look for.

Just don't go for the ones that say 'broadminded person required'. This means you can expect to see two giant dykes washing their overalls in the bath and cutting their hair in the kitchen.

Or some bloke going out the door wearing a wig and a dress and when you come home one night he and all his mates are porking each other in the living room dressed up as sea-scouts.

But you find ones to suit your needs. And where else could an old Bondi boy live? So after checking out six lemons I found one. Right on the beach with great views, security building, garage and pool — $110 a week. My room was about equal to what a junior officer would get in a Soviet army barracks but the kitchen was right on Campbell Parade with a top perv on the chicks walking past, and the landlady and Megadeth, my fellow boarder, seemed amicable enough.

Bright lights, big city, Bobby baby's back in town. I paid my bond and moved in.

All the time I was looking for a flat the weather was fantastic.

The day I moved in a monstrous storm hit and it never stopped raining for a week.

The first night I spent in a mouldy sleeping bag on a mattress that felt like it was full of riverstones and just as cold. I got an electric blanket and a doona the next day but it was still cold and raining and my play was set in Sydney in Spring. The TV in the flat was ordinary with bad reception and being number three in the pecking order meant no *7.30 Report, Four Corners* or *Murphy Brown.*

Plus there was no stereo and it kept on raining. By week two this was becoming as inspirational as one of John Hewson's speeches in Parliament.

But there was one small ray of sunshine. The garage was huge and full of junk and when I was fossicking around for another mattress, what should I find?

A 10-speed bike. An old French Gitanes — covered in rust, it had been laying there for years. The landlady didn't know it was there, Megadeth didn't know anything about it, so I took it to a bike shop in Bondi Junction and got it done up for $125. I was like a Viking in Valhalla.

It finally cleared up for two days so I went pedalling around my old hometown. And hasn't Bondi changed? And don't the motorists in Sydney love you?

In Terrigal, when I walk out the front all I see are a few magpies walking around and sometimes a kookaburra sitting on my letter-box.

In Bondi, it took me 10 minutes just to cross the street. Forget pedestrian crossings. Drivers hate them almost as much as they hate you on a pushbike.

But I cruised around while the sun was out. Bondi's sure changed in the past few years. It's now sort of super trendsville at one end and sleaze at the other. The old Astra Hotel, where they used to drag the junkies out of the brascoes with picks hanging out of their arms, is gone.

Apart from the Bondi Hotel, you don't do pub crawls any more. You do cappuccino-with-a-twist crawls. Bondi's now all coffee shops and alfresco restaurants or trattorias. They're all very 'okay-yar-darling'.

The Italian one where the Astra used to be is good but I would say the yuppie mecca would be the Lamrock Café, right on the corner of the street I grew up in. That's the place to be seen with your cellular phone in your Bottega Veneta briefcase. Wearing your Giorgio Armani sunglasses, Hugo Boss silk shirt and Redealli jacket. Or your Giorgio di Sant'Angelo dress, Betsey Johnson black stockings and Reena Pachochi earrings. While you eat soya noodles, Kiwi fruit sorbet and sip champagne with cranberry sauce and peach schnapps.

If that doesn't turn you on, you can drop some ecky then shoot down to the Bondi and dance to house music at 1000km/h.

I bought an old stereo down from Terrigal for the flat to play my zydeco tapes and the landlady her Black Box and Madonna collection. Then the other boarder, who I nicknamed Megadeth because he never had the band's T-shirt off his back, hit it with Anthrax, Atomic Dustbin, Motorhead etc., till the speakers looked like a couple of old safes after Darcy Dugan had blown them.

But I persevered with the weather and settled back ready to write the next great Australian play. That's when it all fell in a heap. I got pissed one night, forgot my pin number and the machine kept my card, leaving me broke. The clutch went in my car leaving me stranded in Terrigal — 'We're doing our best mate but the part's gotta come up from Sydney.'

Then, when I get back with my spare typewriter and table all keen as a bean, the landlady hits me and Megadeth with the good news. She's not renewing the lease. She's found greener pastures and she's moving on. We could do our best. The Salvos, the Matt Talbot home, the garage if we wanted or we could take over the lease for around $2500.

We got two weeks to make up our mind. I'd barely moved in, put up with the lowest weather imaginable and almost sent myself broke. And now, on the threshold of becoming a famous playwright, I'm out on the street.

They're all right, Australian sheilas. Don't you worry about that. But, as me and Megadeth said one night while we were drinking away our pain, what the landlady did to us will be on her conscience for the rest of her life.

So as I write this I'm being turfed out of my Bondi digs a lot poorer and definitely no wiser. Back to the beautiful Central Coast after roasting all the local coppers and slagging the local beauty queen.

But in times of trouble, I've always got my mate Wally who owns the hot-dog shop down at Peppers to fall back on for a bit of solace.

I was in there the other day having a coffee and showing him my new 10-speed. I couldn't tell him the whole thing in Bondi had fallen in a huge pile of shit. I just said I'd decided to move back home.

Wally looked at me. Looked at the bike, shook his head and said: 'Jesus you're a lucky bastard, Barrett. That's gotta be the best bike for the money in Australia.'

I worked it out. Seven weeks at $110 a week, plus the $125 to get it done up and several grapefruit sorbets, cappuccinos and bottles of Acacia at various bistros in Campbell Parade.

He's gotta be #%*&! joking, hasn't he?

KAKADU, the NEW EDEN

If there's one thing I hate and will not condone it's cruelty to animals for entertainment or profit — especially native fauna, but it goes for anything.

I saw something on TV the other night that just about made me spew. A bunch of redneck Seppos somewhere in Texas got a young black leopard that had been bred in captivity, took it to a clearing, let it out of its cage — then shot it.

The poor bloody thing was no more than an overgrown house cat that had been declawed.

They forced the terrified animal out of the cage. It crawled under a car and they set a pack of dogs on it. Then some all-American hero in a cammy jacket and a baseball cap went over and shot it.

The thing never had a chance. All this rare, beautiful animal got was five minutes of agony and terror before the Seppo jerk put a bullet in it.

That was bad enough. But then this heroic Marlboro man got a video and photos of him sitting next to it with his gun and all his Seppo mates are going, 'Hey, yeah, wow! Goddamn! You did it, Chuck baby. Sonofabitch!'

And they're all shaking hands and posing like this mort's dock with ears had accomplished some great feat of daring.

What do they say? Only in America?

No wonder Australians poke shit at them all the time. It was an absolutely disgusting scene. Now I know why Derryn Hinch looks like he's got bowel trouble all the time, having to see things like this. But good luck to old pumpkin head for bringing these outrages to the public's attention.

Cruelty to animals comes in all ways besides a bunch of gun-crazy Seppos. Greyhound owners use live possums to blood their dogs. Blokes seem to think it's macho to set two dogs on each other or if their dog almost rips some poor little kid's face off.

Pitt Street farmers leave horses to starve on properties. Silly old sheilas think it's just innocent fun if their moggie rips a Willie wagtail or a lorikeet to bits.

I'm not saying I'm holier than thou or completely innocent as far as cruelty to animals goes — apart from when I used to work in the slaughteryards.

Many's the time I kneed Rosie in the kidneys when I'd find her on the bed, farting her head off with the electric blanket on.

I let Achmet in one freezing cold night and he returned my hospitality by dumping in the bath. I kicked his ring that far up his arse and out the front door he was wearing it for a flea collar for the next two weeks.

And when I was working at Ross River in Townsville we used to do some terrible things with firecrackers to cane toads.

They used to swarm in our backyard so we fed them lighted bungers, or tied them to their backs with rubber bands and made bets to see how far they got before they blew themselves to bits. Sadistic, low bastards we were.

And we thought it was hilarious, till a few of them hopped into the kitchen and it looked like an IRA bombing gone wrong all over the walls of the house. After that we got more humane and just shot them with air rifles.

But who likes cane toads anyway? Especially if you follow rugby league and come from NSW.

Circuses often come in for a bagging. People want to get them banned or something along those lines. I'm afraid I have to agree with that to a certain extent.

Not that I'd ban circuses completely. Trapeze acts, knife-throwing clowns etc. are funny and daring acts performed by fit and skilful people. But I'll go along with banning animal acts — apart from maybe dogs and horses.

The circus came to Gosford last summer. I was walking across the park to catch a train and it was 40 degrees Celsius.

And there were these lions and tigers stuck in a metal cage at noon in the middle of Summer. They were nothing more than glorified birdcages. I was 50m away and they stank.

The best these animals can hope for is to get forced into a bigger birdcage every now and again and have some bloke looking like a cross between Jungle Jim and a Polish fireman cracking whips and making them jump through hoops of fire. Okay, Captain Schultz is game getting into a cage with a few lions and tigers, but big deal.

Then outside I noticed these poor bloody elephants shuffling around in circles, bare chains locked around their legs. Not a very inspiring sight I thought.

A spokesman for some circus said, 'Yeah, but these animals don't know any other life.' He was only talking through his pocket.

I reckon the animals are entitled to know a better existence than spending their life in a cage or the world's smallest remand yard. I reckon if they pissed animal acts off from circuses and showed more clowns and acts of daring they'd get more punters anyway.

Who wants to see a lot of tired, smelly animals doing things God never intended them to do? We might as well go back to the days of the Roman Colosseum, set the things on each other, then kill the survivors.

That'd go over well with the kids. Like bullfights and fox and stag hunting. Marlin fishing's starting to get a bit that way too if you ask me.

I'm not saying all sport to do with animals is cruel, like horseracing, trotting etc.

And I definitely don't think rodeos are cruel. The other way around if anything. Any man or woman that's game enough to get on a bull like Chainsaw or Freddie Krueger and risk getting stomped on or having half a lung ripped out has got a heart as big as a football.

In fact, I wouldn't mind coming back as a rodeo bull in the afterlife. All you do is roam around a big paddock in the sun rooting yourself silly and eating your head off.

And to earn your keep you just go out and belt the shit out of some bloke in a big hat and a belt buckle that's really given you the shits for getting up on your back when you could be at home porking, eating and getting into a bit of James Blundell on your Walkman.

I have to give it to rodeo riders though. Jesus, they're good styles of blokes and they must get some sheilas — plus they've got a terrific attitude towards life. No LA Gear tracksuits or $300 Reebok cross-trainers needed for these blokes to keep fit.

No, I figure it's about time we started doing the animals a favour for a change. If we don't start getting our shit together there'll be none left at all.

Overpopulation is what's stuffing the planet: we could do with more wildlife and less people. But try telling that to the Pope. Which is why I get involved with saving animals rather than starving people.

Okay, those films coming out of Ethiopia and Bangladesh are horrifying. But how do governments equate those scenes with the French sitting on food mountains in Europe and Australians shooting and burying 100 million sides of lamb?

I was talking with some like-minded punters and we came up with what I thought wasn't a bad idea.

What have we got in Australia? One of the biggest national parks in the world — Kakadu. Guarded by the spirit of Bulla.

And who is the greatest PM this country or the world has ever seen? Robert James Lee Hawke. Bob to his mates.

What are some of the animals most in danger at present? Elephants, rhinos and hippos.

Poachers kill them so the rotten Japanese can make ivory-combs. The silly bloody Chinese are convinced eating ground-up rhino horn will give you a bigger dick. And the Arabs like hippo teeth for dagger handles. The list goes on and on.

What would be wrong with letting, say, 50 of each animal roam around in a part of Kakadu away from the crocodiles? They couldn't do any more damage than all the buffalo up there. And have the Kooris look after them.

Toss in a few orang-outangs and pandas too. This wouldn't be just the world's greatest national park, it could be the new Garden of Eden — protected by Bulla and looked after by our indigenous people with the white's help.

Okay, so we're introducing an alien species — but the animals would soon sort out what and what not to eat and if it didn't work we could move them onto reserves.

Money? Christ. If we can afford to give the Abos on Arukun $30 million a year to get pissed and find $72 million to arrest a few old war criminals we could give this a go.

The thing is, if it worked it could turn out to be the biggest tourist attraction in the world and net billions. Forget about stuffing up our coastline for silly bloody resorts. We're talking big bikkies here.

And what would we call this modern-day wonder that would exist in perpetuity like Mount Rushmore and the Pyramids? The Robert James Lee Hawke Heritage National Park. The greatest Prime Minister Australia's ever seen. The man who did it all for Bulla.

I reckon Bonzer'll go for it. A lot of people out there will say I'm just pandering to the PM's ego. I don't reckon Bob Hawke's got an ego. But what's the betting 10 years from now there are more elephants and endangered species roaming around Kakadu than you can poke an Instamatic at.

A Garden of Eden created by Bob. Why shouldn't he give us the national park we deserve? It couldn't be worse than the recession we had to have.

The REPUBLIC starts to FLAG

It's on, and I mean on! Is we is or is we ain't gonna be a republic?

The tanks are rumbling in the village square. The banana growers are getting ready to cash in. The battle lines are drawn.

The Bruce Ruxtons etc. on one side and the eminent people on the other, like Mark Day — you know him, from the Melbourne *Truth*.

Even Wavenous Won Casey and Stormin' Normie Rowe slugged it out on prime-time TV. What's the next event? Thomas Keneally v John Howard? What a shitfight this is turning into already, and we've hardly even started debating whether or not Australia should become a republic.

But, if we do what the Yanks did and break free from the shackles of colonialism, the first thing we have to do is piss off the monarchy.

Bring out the tumbrels, sharpen up the guillotine, off with their perfumed, sequined heads; the bludgers are 20,000km away, for a start.

But hang on a minute. This republicanism is a lot easier said than done, and I've got a bit to lose here if we give old Betty Boo and her kinsfolk the lemon.

Okay, so bleary-eyed and still hungover I got up one week to watch *Sunday* on Channel Nine and found out the Queen makes $3 million a day and doesn't pay any taxes.

This seems a bit iffy. I might own a couple of dressing-gowns and I can be a bit of a boring old fart now and again, but I'm definitely not a queen. I've met quite a number in the entertainment industry and they pay taxes.

How come Liz baby doesn't have to weigh in? She's a billionaire with an art and jewel collection that's incalculable in value. Yet we commoners are expected to support her, the Governor General and various Governors all over Australia. Like the late Sir John Kerr. And didn't he need a bit of support at the 1977 Melbourne Cup?

Then we got Bill Hayden plus a team of flunkies that kept him and them in a style that's unimaginable.

I'll bet he never had it that good when he was in the Queensland wallopers.

Is it worth all the millions of dollars to retain the monarchy and all the hangers-on? Once we go republican they're gone forever.

There's no doubt the monarchy does set a standard of speech and manners that's incomparable. Good upper-class Pommies are without peer and the way they look down their noses at commoners is exquisite. They're almost worth keeping just for snob value.

And poor Prince Charles. He's such a wimp, how could you get rid of him? It'd be like putting down the family dog.

Then there's Ita Buttrose and the rest of the gushettes from the women's magazines. Imagine *New Idea* and *Woman's Day* without a royal wedding or a royal baby or a royal bowel movement to report on.

It could mean the end of women's magazines in Australia altogether, taking all those employees with them.

It might be an idea to maintain the monarchy, if not just for Bruce Ruxton and the Tallangatta ladies' auxiliary bowls club, at least for the employees of *New Idea*.

Then there's my end. As I said in a previous column, if Chilla becomes King it's a public holiday on his birthday, same day as mine, and I promised myself I could get blind, rotten, face-down-in-the-gutter drunk with the dogs pissing on my swag on November 14 and it'd all be sweet.

That's out the bloody door. Become a republic maybe, but retain the monarchy just for Charlie and Bob on our birthday. The King and I.

But what say, when it comes to the crunch, the Poms say no, you can't have a republic and send in the RAF and the Ghurkhas, and we have to have another Eureka Stockade? Even if prominent MP and author Jeffrey Archer says we should become a republic.

There'll be casualties, billions of dollars worth of damage to Australia's infrastructure. We could finish up like Iraq. Like I said, this going republican is a lot easier said than done.

But the fighting and ruination of what little economy we've got left is the easy part. Because what it all boils down to is, if we dump the monarchy and go for a republic we have to change the flag.

In other words, dump the Union Jack. What are we going to replace it with that doesn't offend anybody? A minority group, no-one, not a single solitary soul.

As we all know, especially if you're a white Australian heterosexual, you can't say anything about anyone these days without it either being racist, sexist, demeaning, patronising or offending.

So you tell me, in this climate of multiculturalism and gay rights, what we're going to replace the Union Jack with that doesn't either offend or encroach on someone's rights or sensitivities.

Okay, we leave the Southern Cross there. No-one, not even the North Queenslanders, would have a moan about Australia being referred to as the land of the Southern Cross.

But what goes in the corner? A kangaroo? No. That would offend environmentalists. How could you put a national symbol on the flag and then shoot four million a year for dog food?

What about a koala? No. In 10 years the only koalas you'll see will be in Japanese zoos. There was a small colony left in Sydney, but the Government sold the land to an Indonesian businessman and he bulldozed all the trees to build houses.

How about we put on a wok and crossed chopsticks to please all our Asian migrants? That would offend the Muslims. So we add the green crescent of Islam in respect to Allah — peace and blessings upon his name.

But which Muslims? The Sunnis? The Shi'ites? The Cherokee, Blackfoot or Sioux Muslims? You're on very shaky ground here. And this would offend the Jews. All right, we'll shove in the Star of David.

But this would offend all the other Arabs. Plus the neo-Nazis and the skinheads. They're a minority group. They've got rights too. We'll throw in the towel and paint the bloody thing white.

But then we'd be accused of pandering to the Ku Klux Klan and the Aryan supremacists and that would offend all the other blacks.

Talking about blacks, what about the Kooris? They want their own flag. So the Abos are going to bellow on principle's sake. Even if you threw in a goondie, it's still going to mean 200 years of rape, murder and torture.

What about all the Slavs settled here? They've got a bit of a say, surely. So we put in a bit of red-and-white check to keep the Croatians happy.

But this would offend the Serbs. And what about the Slovenians? Death to the Slovenian dogs. They invaded our village in 1032AD.

What about Transylvanians? There would have to be a lesbian vampire workshop out there being discriminated against. Plus the poofs. They're always being discriminated against.

But gays have got rights, so instead of a flag why not stick to the nicely embroidered quilt with the names of the dearly departed on it?

Did I leave out the Indians and Pakistanis? But which ones? The Hindus? The Brahmans? It's all Sikhs of one and half a dozen of the other over there. I told you, it's not going to be easy changing the flag.

Amongst all this madness and consternation I knew there was only one person to ask. The oracle. My mate Wally, down at Designa-Dogs, the hot-dog shop in Peppers at Terrigal.

A lot of people are starting to wonder who this mysterious Wally is that keeps bobbing up in my column. Like me, Wally's another carpetbagger from the eastern suburbs of Sydney who moved to the Central Coast.

Unlike me, Wally has a small family and is therefore more responsible. Wally is also more wise in the ways of the world than myself, probably because he sees it from behind the great counter of life.

Before he moved here, Wally was a coal-trimmer and captain and president of the Coogee–Randwick Wombats, a top junior league team in Sydney.

The Wombats are legend in Sydney and to become president and captain is no mean feat, which is why in times of trouble I always ask Wally his opinion.

So I said to him: 'Wally, what do you think they should put on the Australian flag where the Union Jack used to be?'

Straightaway, Wally said: 'What's wrong with a wombat?'

I was stunned. A pearl of wisdom, woven from a web of words of pure brilliance. I couldn't think of anything more laconically lucid or sensationally simplistic. Wally had done it again.

Put a wombat in the corner of the flag. That couldn't possibly offend anybody. Wombats are grouse. They're cute and cuddly and they're a protected species. A wombat's like a perfect boarder, just eats roots and leaves. Everybody likes wombats.

They're tough little bastards when it comes to the pinch! Ask anybody who's hit a wombat.

Plus, they have this amazing mating ritual where the male wombat has to run round in circles eight times at night, trying to bite the female on the backside in a special way to get a bit of the other.

And if he doesn't do it right he gets the heave for another wombat. Round and round in circles he goes, getting nowhere.

And isn't that typical of Australian sheilas? They run you round and round in circles till you get giddy, then they give you the lemon.

I couldn't think of anything more typical. Instead of a banana republic, we'd be known as a wombat republic. I couldn't see this offending anyone.

In fact, after watching Wampaging Won Casey slugging it out on television, I think the only ones who'd be offended would be the wombats themselves.

Leave no TURN UNSTONED

I'd be lying if I said there weren't a few lurks, perks and freebies in the publishing rort, whether you're a columnist or an author.

Even I get to the odd turn now and again. Living up here on the Central Coast, I don't get to heaps, and I never seem to see my head in the social pages in the Sunday kite.

Don't expect to find me at the Cointreau Ball or the DJ's fashion launch doing the lambada with Amanda Urquhart or Marie-Caroline Perignon. But if there's a turn on and they mention the magic words 'free piss', I'm there.

However, free piss isn't the be-all and end-all. What's the point of driving 100km to invariably fill up on Tooheys Red, VB or cheap chardonnay — none of which turns me on all that much — and losing your licence on the way home after putting up with boring wombats getting that far into your ear you need a poultice to get them out?

I've been to some good turns and met some nice people. I met NSW Police Minister Ted Pickering at one. He was all right and I had a good mag with him about law and order.

I meant to ask him if he wanted to come back, pull a few cones and get into a bit of Guns'n'Roses, but his minders dragged him away before I got a chance.

I've been to turns that had all the atmosphere of a railway station in Siberia. Been ignored to my face by fellow writers, stabbed in the back. And returned the favour with great zeal and gusto.

I've been buttonholed for off-the-cuff, in-depth interviews. Some woman journo said to me one night, after about an hour of probing: 'But what is it you're trying to say in your book?' I struck an author's pose and replied: 'All I'm trying to say is, if you've got $10, these books aren't a bad read.'

It may not be the quote of the decade, but it got rid of her.

Movie reviews, despite the free piss, can be disastrous, especially if the movie's a giant snail.

I've left theatres where you'd think they just dug a body up from under the floorboards. And you're in it, suffering the slings and arrows of fellow actors worried about their careers.

You just can't get drunk, take the money and run, can you?

Record company launches can be a bit off, too. I haven't been to many — they're not my bag.

I wouldn't know an E flat from a Q plunk and getting a mag on with people in the music industry is spooky. You keep thinking you're talking to a replicant who's just done a bust on an op-shop.

Forget groupies. Tom Cruise couldn't get a groupie at a rock party. They're all waiting for George Michael or Johnny Diesel to come in.

A turn is a turn, though, no matter what. And if someone's good enough to shout you free drink and some nosh, it's a bit vulgar to turn up and carry on like they've just amputated your leg.

But every now and again you get to the grouse. A ripper turn, drinks on the house, top band, good-looking women, nice folks all round.

Yes, Allah, peace and blessings be upon him, finally shone down on this miserable pile of scrapings from between the toes of beggars.

After two years of columns for this illustrious mag, they figured it was safe to invite me to the 1991 Covergirl Of The Year turn.

Was this a party? Was Dresden an air-raid?

It was in the Arizona Bar in a top hotel in Sydney. 'The Happening Thang' played. Frank Vincent, the inflatable sports reporter from the Doug Mulray show, compered and the winner, Kim Rankin, is from the Central Coast. What a combination.

There was no way I was driving back home after this, so I decided to give myself a spoil and book a suite for the night. The CB in Pitt Street, just up from the railway, had a room for a person of my standing. $25 a night. Clean sheets, shower down the hallway, leave your valuables at the desk. When you're muled-out-drunk, a bed's just a bed. And I knew when I threw the towel in I'd sleep under a cow pissing.

The turn started at 6.30 and I got there at ten to, meeting Frank Vincent and the editor of *People* setting things up. On the bar were about 50 pink cocktails of some description, so I thought I'd see how many I could sink in 30 minutes before anyone else got there.

About half-an-hour later the place started to fill up, and 25 strawberry-flavoured tequilas hit me and I could see it was going to be a hoot right from the word go.

Franco Vincenzo got up and did his thing, the editor made a speech, Kim Rankin, looking like $500 million with a smile as wide as the heads, thanked everybody.

The band started. I hit the dance floor with another 10 tequila supernovas under my belt — and didn't I show those young whippersnappers how to dance?

I don't quite know how to describe my style. Sort of a white Doctor Huxtable. No matter what, we were all getting into our stride when the band stopped and a bloke rode in on a horse, all lit up, singing 'Rhinestone Cowboy'.

I've never seen a horse like this. It did everything but tell you the joke about the singing telegram. The flashes going off didn't bother it a bit: I think it thrived on it.

Next up was the rider with a whip, cracking paper from people's mouths. He was that good I volunteered, but he said my nose blocked the light too much.

We got back into the dancing and drank on till they closed the bar. What can I say? I had a top time. Drank, danced and laughed.

A hard core of pisshead journos and their ilk kicked on to keep drinking somewhere else. But Robert G. Barrett, distinguished author, would never have made a very good tent fighter — I know when I've had enough. I staggered back to the Richard Burton suite at the CB and moaned and farted till sun-up.

Did I have a hangover the next day? Yes. The industrial strength, six-Panadeines-at-a-time kind.

Yet I had to hang around Sydney till 4 p.m. So what did I do, just to prove how crooked I was on myself? Went and saw a science fiction movie called *Hardware*.

It was the lowest and loudest movie I've ever wasted $11 on. There's stuff-all story. It's like 2000 of the worst video clips you've ever seen, welded together with blasts of punishing music. Saddam Hussein and Tony 'The Nose' Lambert should be made to sit through this.

But having what was left of my brains scrambled by some horrendous soundtrack was a small price to pay for the night before.

In fact, it was that good I've booked the same room for next year.

An ARTFUL DODGER

Along with the happy ones, I get the odd sad letter now and again.

I got one the other week from a woman in Whalan, NSW, from which I'll quote parts: 'I'm Rikki Taylor's mum, you met me when we lived at Bondi. Rikki has only a few months to live. She and her twin sister were diagnosed terminally ill two years ago. Rikki cared for her sister until she died two weeks ago.'

It goes on: 'We reminisce while I care for her at home until she dies. She speaks fondly of you. I thought you might like to send a message of cheer in your own inimitable way. She reads your column in *People* each week. Sincerely …'

I remember Rikki. She was 22, brownish sort of hair and a good sort. She had a tattoo of a mushroom with a little dwarf on her backside and always used to call me a creep. I liked her and thought we had a bit of a good thing going until she eventually gave me the arse for another bloke.

But one day me and Rikki really burnt all the trendies' and posers' arses at Tamarama beach in Sydney.

It was summer and I had an old flat right on the water. A mate of mine had a big yacht and told me he'd be sailing past at 2 p.m. one crowded Sunday arvo. When the time came I grabbed Rikki, a pair of fins and a surfmat and, with Rikki on my back, jumped off the point and swam out to the yacht.

We climbed on board and sailed down to Maroubra and back. When we got back to Tamarama, we dived off on the surfmat, caught a wave to the beach then strolled casually back to my flat and had a beer.

The poofs and the posers couldn't believe it. It made playing backgammon on the sand in your sequined leather G-string look very predictable and dull.

After I'd read the letter from her mum, I sent my old mate Rikki a letter and thanked her once again for giving me the arse. I still like her even if she did call me a creep all the time.

Then you don't get a letter, you get a phone call from your cousin George: 'Uncle Artie's in Bethlehem hospital with cancer of the pancreas.'

Now, I always dedicate books to people. In one I put 'Ex-painters and dockers and old SP bookies aren't bad blokes — and neither is my Uncle Artie in Melbourne. This book is dedicated to him.'

Let me tell you about my Uncle Artie and why I flew straight down to see one of the grousest blokes who ever lived.

Uncle Art was the Don Corleone of South Melbourne years ago. I was 16 when dad died and Art said come down to Melbourne, he'd take me under his wing.

He'd turned up the SP betting and had a barrow at the South Melbourne markets where I got a job yelling out 'potatoes, peas, beans, tamaataaaas'. I got to meet all these nefarious characters with names like Noodles, Chopsticks and Hoover — who'd pick up anything.

They wore expensive clothes and beautiful shoes, which they used mainly to kick members of other gangs half to death when they weren't shooting them. It wasn't a young surfie's idea of a good time, so I thanked Uncle Art and legged it back to Sydney.

But it was always a big scene when Uncle Art and Auntie Bonnie would come up to visit the family. I was about 10. They'd book into a good hotel and often take me to the zoo or the pictures and I can remember Art saying, 'I might take my rod with me.' I kept expecting us to go fishing, but the kind of rod Art was talking about you'd never see in Paul Kidd's column.

I can remember going out with Uncle Art to visit Uncle Joe Barrett who owned the Leichhardt Wanderers snooker club, and watching them get measured up for new shoulder holsters by this Italian leather worker. Then they blazed away out in the backyard having a few practice runs.

Another vivid memory was when the family jumped in the FJ and drove down to visit him. As I walked in the front of Art's house in South Melbourne, I noticed all these holes in the door and more holes and pieces of plaster ripped out of the wall along the corridor.

'What happened?' I asked.

'I've just had the decorators in,' he replied. At the time, Uncle Art was an official in the Painters and Dockers Union and had misplaced some funds, plus some other chops that had fallen in from somewhere, so — in a show of union solidarity — the P and Ds had driven past the previous night and machine-gunned his house.

Art used to run the SP at the Town Hall Hotel in South Melbourne during and after the war. The cops in town got

30 quid a month and the local cops got a fiver. They'd have 200 punters in the lane with the betting sheets pinned up on the fence.

If by chance some hillbilly cops should appear near the scene, the cockatoos would give Art the drum and all the old sheilas would hide the sheets in their bloomers.

The cops couldn't get a pinch and no mugs could come up after and say, 'But I had such-and-such on so-and-so …'

But could my Uncle Artie pull some beautiful strokes?

During the war he was a brewer with his own boutique label. They used to put the frighteners on some bloke who worked at Corio whisky to sell them a couple of gallons of 100 per cent pure whisky each week. Art would mix this with dry sherry and some boiled currant and methylated spirit brew Auntie Bon mixed up, then he'd flog it to the GIs as Kentucky Suntan Bourbon.

The Yanks couldn't get enough of it, especially the blacks — which was where Artie got the name.

Uncle Artie wanted to serve his country but being a P and D he was in an essential industry and had a national security card. Unfortunately, he somehow finished up with more national security cards than he needed, so he released some to a few friends — and consequently got arrested by the military police for being such a good bloke.

Art would have spent the war as a guest of His Majesty only Ben Chifley signed his bail slip. Ben could always get set on the nod with Uncle Art, no worries, as they're apt to say in Melbourne.

Naturally, being a survivor from the painters and dockers wars, Art was invited to the wake for Jack 'Putty Nose' Nicholls.

But he'd been out of circulation for a while and said to one of the officials at his table: 'I'm sorry to hear about Putty Nose.

I didn't even know he was sick. When did he die?' And the official from the union said, 'Tomorrow.'

There's heaps more to Uncle Art than that. Besides, he's family and I love him, even if he was a bit of an old villain.

I don't know if many Ps and Ds read this column but if there are any, how about ducking out to Caulfield. Art's in Bethlehem hospital, and he deserves respect.

I'm PULLING for ya, PEE WEE

People wonder why I take shots at Americans in my column. Am I anti-American? Not really. It's just that, at times, Seppos are so thick.

They can never tell when you're joking with them and it's almost impossible for Yanks to take the piss out of themselves. Maybe they should learn — then they wouldn't spend millions on analysts and gurus.

Of all those American sheilas who wrote to me, I narrowed the field down to two you could have a joke with — in New York and in Carolina.

I also write to an American photographer who lives in Sarasota, Florida. I met him through another photographer. He's not a bad bloke and stayed with me when he was out here making a TV doco on Aboriginal cave paintings.

But he was strapped for a sense of humour and we nicknamed him Joyce. Like in Wendy Harmer's book, *It's A Joke, Joyce*.

I still write to him, send him books and that, but no matter what I say, he almost always blows up and drowns me with letters bagging Australia and Australians. Like I said, he's not a bad bloke, but I just can't figure him out.

I picked up the *Sydney Morning Herald* the other week and in someone's column, rating about three paragraphs, was how Pee Wee Herman got arrested in Sarasota, Florida, for having a three-bags-full in the back of the local pictures. Which was about all it was worth.

Next thing, all these clippings out of US newspapers arrive from Joyce. Pee Wee's tug in the South Trail Adult Theatre, 6700 Block Street, made headlines in the *Sarasota Herald Tribune* and just about every other paper in the country.

I couldn't believe it. If, say, Daryl Somers' ostrich got nabbed flogging himself in the Avoca Theatre I couldn't see it making the *Central Coast Express*.

But in America it's banner headlines. 'Pee Wee's case raised old issue' howled one. 'Policing morality' was another one. 'It's a matter of image' shrieked another.

Punters and celebrities jumped to his defence. 'They are judging the man without right of due process,' was blazed above a photo of Bill Cosby.

They've got a raging crack problem and the Soviet Union's going to hell along with Yugoslavia. Pee Wee gets caught pulling his pud and it's headlines and they rally into the street holding petitions.

That's Seppos for you.

Naturally, I had to reply to Joyce's letter. I didn't quite know how to approach this, so I thought the best thing would be to take the offensive. Joyce had invited me over to his neck of the woods in return for staying at my place while he was out here once. Not after this, though.

What sort of backward, hillbilly joint do you live in, I demanded? Do you mean to tell me that if I go to see *In Bed With Madonna* or *9½ Weeks* and I crack it for a larrikin, I can't have a three-bagger?

What sort of dump are you running over there? What about MY image? What about if my analyst says it's good therapy for me to have a nice relaxing J. Arthur Rank at the movies? Do I get persecuted too, like poor Pee Wee? It's disgraceful. What the %$#@!'s going on?

Besides, I wrote, isn't it every American's constitutional right to get around having a wank? You've been wanking non-stop for years in your letters and you've never been pinched.

Where's the equality and justice?

I remembered how much Yanks like to turn a dollar and adore celebrity status. So I sent him a few dollars and told him to go buy the seat where Pee Wee got caught with a full hand, going alone.

Yanks dig these sort of things — like the door where John Lennon got shot, Madonna's corsets, etc.

It could be worth anything at the start of Pee Wee's trial. I addressed the letter to Joyce so-and-so, Stropisota, Florida, Three Bagging Capital of America — and wished him the best.

Back came the first letter like a Nike missile. When are all we moron Australian sonsofbitches ever going to learn, it said. We copy everything Americans do. We're jealous because America's always ahead of us. We creep into the USA, soak up as much Americana as possible, then write belittling, disparaging things out of jealousy.

I'm a pinhead, we're all slushpumps, living in a pitifully barren entertainment scene. We need guidance, we should be nuked. Bleah, bleah, bleah! What did I do wrong?

All I did was sympathise with Pee Wee, agree with Bill Cosby and ask him to save me a seat at the local pictures. Fair dinkum — you'd get more laughs from the *Egyptian Book of the Dead* than you would out of Joyce's letters.

Which for some reason brings me to blonde jokes. The latest bunch of offensive, sexist gags to surface in which blonde women are made out to be giggling bimbos.

And where else would you hear these? From that odious, balding gnome who does the breakfast show on 2MMM, Doug Mulray.

Mulray fancied himself as a preacher — the Rev. Dr Doug he called himself. I wonder what religious order he represented — The Church of the Immaculate Flatophile?

'Lay your hands on the radio my children,' he said. Yeah … it'd probably just go phhhhhhhtttt! Some deacon. The wrath of Jehovah will surely be upon the head of this blasphemer. Yea, it is written: fart jokes are an abomination and lay off women — especially blondes.

Anyway, when I tuned into the Rev. Dr Doug I was expecting a bit of good old religion. And what did I get? Blonde jokes. On they came — and each as offensive and sexist as the other.

Then I had a thought: 'I might not be as quick-witted as the ex-Rev. Dr Doug or good enough to be a writer on his show, but I can be just as sexist and repulsive as that little bandersnatch any day.'

And I can write a blonde joke.

So, in the light of recent circumstances, here is my first go at a blonde joke: Why would you rather go to the pictures with Pee Wee Herman than a blonde? Because Pee Wee Herman doesn't talk during the movie.

I SAW that and I'm TELLING

Remember that horrible kid at school everyone hated — the class tittle-tat?

Always dobbing. Always going: 'Oowhah! I saw that and I'm telling.'

You couldn't belt him, because every time you did he'd run crying to the teacher and you'd get caned.

But we sorted out the one in our class — every sports afternoon, we'd pick the locks of his school case and shit in it. It was beautiful to watch when he'd open his case, go 'oowhah!', then cry when he'd find a big, steaming mockingbird in amongst his schoolbooks.

Something resembling that kid at school is hosting a show on the ABC called *Media Watch* — Stuart Littlemore.

I've watched about as much of this show as I can stomach — and only that much because it comes on straight after *Four Corners*, and the Monday night movies on the other channels are usually stuffed.

It's 15 minutes of carping, insipid negativism from what would have to be the most droning, somniferous voice on TV. Vocal Serapax.

It's hard to imagine anybody could bore the tits off you in such a short space of time, but Littlemore does it with ease. This moralising, holier-than-thou's idea of entertainment is to go through the papers and TV news shows nit-picking for any puerile solecism or anything he deems remotely sexist, racist or humorous.

You'd only get a show like this amongst the flat-earthers on the ABC — the network that brought you Trish Goddard, *Racket,* Jane Singleton, etc. Out in the real world I reckon Littlemore would find the going a lot tougher.

He's always putting the boot into the Packer and Murdoch press and just about everybody else, but the bottom line is that Littlemore's like the parrot on the biscuit tin — not quite in it.

I don't reckon the private sector media would wear him if he was a mink coat, so he knocks it, constantly targeting Derryn Hinch and Jana Wendt for his fatuous, prosaic criticism.

Okay, I wouldn't fancy living next door to Hinch. But you never see a word on Littlemore's show about Hinch going into bat for abused kids or Greenpeace. Or about when Jana's *A Current Affair* exposes crooked cops, bastards ripping off pensioners, or the plight of farmers getting thrown off their land. They get no credit for this — just a constant barrage of pedantry from Stu-baby.

Okay, an example: Hinch showed a couple of Parks and Wildlife officers trying to arrest this Asian caught with buckets of undersize shellfish.

This little ingrate had just stripped a reef of everything growing on it, completely stuffing the ecology of the area, and then he puts on the old 'solly no spik English' dodge, to the complete frustration of the two Wildlife officers.

'Pity they couldn't catch some big fish,' sniggered sanctimonious Littlemore. It's a wonder he didn't accuse them of racism.

And the week before when *ACA* tracked Christopher Skase to his villa in Spain, sprung him in a restaurant living it up and buttonholed the so-called bankrupt for an interview, even following him to his taxi as he tried to scuttle away, Littlemore jumped on them.

'Oowhah!' he cried. 'Look at that. TV journalism almost to the point of assault. Tch-tch-tch.' Don't worry about all the poor punters Skase has dudded, Stu. Worry about his right to privacy.

And if any cartoonist makes the slightest gag about women, Littlemore howls sexism. Yet in August he ran a clip from a W.C. Fields movie in which W.C. and a barman are talking about a woman they beat up.

The barman says: 'I knocked her down.' And W.C. says: 'But I was the first one to kick her.'

Littlemore must have thought this hilarious. His face actually moved and he arched an eyebrow. If Littlemore thinks jokes about women getting beaten up are funny, he should visit a casualty ward after some drunken husband's gone to town on his wife.

But Littlemore wants to be very careful with his 15 minutes on Aunty. If a zealot from the Anti-Discrimination Thought Police took a good look at *Media Watch* they could possibly construe it as being racist, sexist, fascist and offensive.

The ADTP could say it's racist because it's spoken in English and the media under scrutiny uses mainly English.

What about some *Media Watch* from *Il Globo, Kosmos, The Maltese Herald* or *Al Fatah*?

Aren't we a multicultural society? Isn't this discrimination against the ethnic media — in other words, racism?

You could say *Media Watch* is sexist because a man hosts it. And aren't all men potential rapists? I've seen women marching under banners saying so.

So why doesn't Littlemore co-host his show with a lesbian? I wouldn't mind my eight cents a day going to see some ugly dyke alongside him.

She couldn't look any more repulsive than his tie collection does.

Then the ADTP could say *Media Watch* is fascist because it's possible there are more right-handed people than left-handed people in Littlemore's production crew. The left is being discriminated against by the right — underhanded fascism.

The ADTP might say *Media Watch* is offensive because Littlemore never wears a jacket. Other gentlemen on the ABC wear jackets. Even Johnny Peard and Arthur Beetson — the Laurel and Hardy of football commentators — wear jackets.

But not Littlemore. He just sits there in his shirtsleeves looking like a bongo drum wearing glasses.

It's possible conservative ABC viewers would find this grossly offensive.

So that's *Media Watch* — I'm not saying it's racist, fascist, offensive *or* sexist — just that it's a boring, pedantic, non-event and another waste of taxpayers' money.

And I'm happier than ever that me and George Gukatis shit in that kid's school case back at Randwick Boys' High.

DR DOUG meets his MATCH

Loath as I am to admit it, I once got sprung having a bludge and watching the *Ray Martin Show*.

The Inbred Construction Co. of Terrigal was laying a concrete drive out the front of my house. Anyone who thinks two heads are better than one has never seen the ICC in action.

I could take no more so I went inside to watch Ray Martin.

Actually, the other reason I was watching the *Ray Martin Show* was because earlier I just happened to be tuned into Doug Mulray on 2MMM. I'm not a Doug Mulray fan — I detest him and I'm sick of mentioning the odious little toad's name.

But I wanted to catch the Rev. Dr Doug's version of *Fractured Fairy Tales*. He mentioned he was compering for Ray Martin that day and his special guest was Leslie Nielsen, star of the two *Naked Gun* movies.

I've seen some funny things on the box over the past few weeks but this was the funniest, most uplifting 90 minutes of TV I've seen in 10 years. Not so much because of Doug Mulray's brilliant wit and rapier-like riposte, but to see the reprehensible little monster get completely done at his own game. He died by his own sword.

Doug Mulray, king of the fart jokes, lord of the noisy rings, got skewered — and then turned into cat meat. Made to look like a fool. And worse, by a Seppo.

No matter what I see again, it was worth heaps to see Leslie Nielsen vaporise Mulray to dust on prime-time TV. And I'm a patriot who hates to see good Aussie boys get done by Yanks.

The show started with the usual razzmatazz and Mullos brushed up okay in a nice shirt and jeans and, with his well-spoken, mellow tones, he soon had the audience eating out of the palm of his hand.

It was pleasant banter for a while. Then, naturally enough, the Rev. Dr Doug slipped out a fart. A reasonable fart which went over well in the studio.

There was a ripple of polite applause from the audience and guffaws, I imagine, in millions of loungerooms across Australia. As an off-the-cuff horse-and-cart, I'd give it a six.

There was more banter, then Mullos introduced his first guest — Leslie Nielsen, who came on with about five metres of toilet paper hanging out of his trousers. This went over enormously because he was so sincerely apologetic about it.

They proceeded to chat away, showed some clips from Nielsen's latest movie and discussed their prostate and stomach problems.

It was nice and cosy, almost tea-with-the-vicar stuff. Then Mulray squeezed out another fart. Not as good as the first one but a reasonable enough effort.

The American took it in his stride like an old pro and they proceeded with the chat. Then Nielsen farted, apologised and kept talking.

Cool as a cucumber.

It was totally unexpected, a complete bolt out of the blue — though you must remember he's 60-odd and you'd expect a bit of flatulence.

As far as I was concerned, and the rest of Australia, he had fluffed on prime-time TV.

Mulray was gone to Gowings. He did his best to regain his composure and there was more tea with the vicar, but the Rev. Dr Doug was staggering.

Then, just as Mullos looked like coming good, Nielsen farted again. A definite nine this time. It blew Mulray completely out of the water. It was cruel in a way, because he was now up against a master.

Nielsen apologised again and took over the show. Doug was gone.

Eventually Mulray had to piss the American off — he was just too good. Mulray was so humbled he even had to produce an old, perished fart cushion from his pants that looked like someone had brought it back from the battle of the Somme. What a cop-out.

Nielsen had Mulray on toast and could have completely vanquished the evil one for all time. But top bloke that he is, he produced what looked like a long, skinny squash ball he had hidden in his hand.

The man is a genius. The Rev. Dr Doug had to sit there like a Lowes dummy as it was exit stage right for the Swamp Fox. What a guy.

But I'm not a complete nark, I'll give credit where it's due. The kid recovered. Mulray's a pro and he got his shit together.

The show proceeded with a band called the 'Fargone Beauties' who play trash bluegrass music. They certainly trashed 'Wild Thing'. They left it looking like rats had chewed it.

I don't know much about trash bluegrass but if it means good-time music by complete hounds of musicians, it's okay by me.

Next was the rugby league player Fatty Vautin and Aussie Rules man Dermo Brereton to discuss the upcoming grand finals and that. Dermo was supposed to be in the studio but they were forced to do a hook-up because the Melbourne genius had missed his plane.

'Couldn't you find your earring?' asked Fatty.

Not a bad bit of repartee for a Queenslander. They chatted for a while but I think neither wished to overtax his mental capacity.

Then Mulray introduced a panel of four delightful women from Melbourne and Sydney. Well-groomed, intelligent, quite attractive, if that's not a sexist remark.

There were two brunettes and two blondes — with the Rev. Dr Doug in the middle — and the subject was, loosely, blonde jokes.

Being the challengers, the brunettes led with a quote from the Oxford dictionary: 'Blonde means light-headed and big boobs,' meowed one brunette. But this, along with everything else, went over okay.

There was no hissing or scratching. No drinks were thrown. No-one copped an Oroton handbag across the jaw. It was all good fun and great verbal riposte.

I'd give the debate to the blondes. They were cool under fire, especially one who was a new mother.

In fact, I'd give the day to the wholesome blonde on the end. And naturally, being a woman, she got the last word in.

She just laughed and said: 'Hey, I got flown up from Melbourne to do this.' And have a good time, too, I imagine.

Which seems to suggest the women in Melbourne are a lot smarter than the men. Even the blondes. At least they can catch a plane.

It was a top ending to a top show and great TV all round. Even if poor Doug got beaten at his own game.

Still, if you live by the fart joke, you die by the fart joke.

DIGGER drops a BOMBSHELL

One of the journos at *People*, Dan Lane, is compiling a book on the experiences of old Aussie diggers, mainly during World War II.

He's been interviewing diggers all over Australia and collecting research on never-before-told stories and, from what Dan tells me, the book should be a ripper.

Oddly enough, I got onto a great story from WWII two doors up the road. From my old mate and neighbour, Norman Taylor.

I like Norm and his wife Dorothy — they were probably the only people in the street who didn't want to have me tarred and feathered when I first moved in. And I know Norm didn't sign the petition 'Ratboy' took to Gosford council over me playing a portable radio on my sundeck.

He and his wife are always laughing and smiling as they work on their substantial block of land which they've almost turned into a nature reserve. And I have to laugh when he tells me about the family of bush turkeys he feeds and the dragon lizards and magpies that follow him around like pets.

I found out Norm is an ex-seaman who'd also moved up from Sydney — same as wharfies and P and Ds, they're down-to-earth, knockabout blokes.

Then one day he told me how he was the only survivor out of 1200 seamen — including the 47 men on his ship — when the Germans bombed Bari Harbour in Italy in 1943, in what was one of the best-kept secrets of WWII.

It was a disaster second only to Pearl Harbor and it was 30 years before the story came out in a book, by US Air Force officer Glenn B. Infield, called just that — *Disaster at Bari.*

Norm was 24 at the time and 3rd engineer on the 'Test Bank' out of England. They'd just been running supplies in and out of Malta, losing eight ships from their last convoy to U-boats.

On December 2 they were in Bari Harbour, empty and waiting to take on supplies. Early that day a lone ME210 reconnaissance plane buzzed the harbour, but no-one took a great deal of notice.

They did at eight o'clock that night, though, when the Luftwaffe arrived with 105 Junker bombers.

From the photos Norm showed me, Bari's like a big version of Coffs Harbour with a long breakwater running right around it. There were 30 ships crammed in there, some of them side by side and the German bombers couldn't miss.

Ship after ship disintegrated, illuminated by the parachute flares dropped by the Germans. Other fires leapt across ships loaded with octane fuel bombs and ammunition.

One ship, the *John B. Motley* — a fuel carrier, took a bomb down the smokestack which, according to Infield's book, 'sent a cloud of exploding fuel 1000 feet into the sky. The entire harbour seemed to empty as the tidal wave caused by the explosion washed over the breakwater'.

Norm's ship took a direct hit in the forward hold, killing nearly every man on board. Norm and three others somehow managed to get a raft into the water and paddled like mad towards the harbour wall.

According to Norm, the noise and the huge waves from the bombs made them feel as if they were in some vicious storm. As they got to the wall, a bomb landed in the water next to them, blowing them eight metres into the air and up onto the dock.

They tumbled out of the raft as another bomb hit, blowing Norm and his mate 20m along the wharf and underneath a truck. The other two got blown back into the water.

Despite the terrific blast from the *Motley*, there were still hundreds of men swimming around in the harbour, including Norm's two mates, and they still had a chance of making it.

But what the allies didn't tell anyone was that another ship, the *John Harvey*, was carrying 100 tonnes of mustard gas bombs. It took two direct hits and thousands of litres of liquid poured into the harbour where the survivors were trying to make shore.

Now they weren't only getting pounded by the Germans, they were choking to death from their own gas. If the *John Harvey*'s load had been known, the ship would have been kept outside the breakwater.

After that it was just carnage, according to Norm. He grabbed his mate's leg to pull him further under the truck, but all he got was a boot with a foot in it. Where the rest of him was, he didn't know.

The bombing lasted an hour. When it stopped, Norm crawled out from beneath the truck and there was nothing but bodies, flames and this eerie, black silence. Shocked and chilled to the bone, he staggered up to a picture theatre, smashed his way in, rolled himself up in one of the stage curtains and collapsed.

The next day, still covered in oil, his clothes in tatters, he joined what land-based survivors there were and headed for first aid.

A group of airmen from 23 RAF squadron gave him a lift and at first thought he was an Italian.

Despite what had happened, Norm scarcely had a scratch, but all around him were people with their skin hanging off, eyes watering, coughing and the doctors and nurses didn't know how to treat them because they didn't know the symptoms of mustard gas poisoning. They put it down as NYD (not yet diagnosed) dermatitis cases.

General Alexander sent a report to Churchill, who refused to believe there were gas casualties.

'The symptoms do not sound like mustard gas,' he said.

But Axis Sally, the Nazi radio propagandist, knew the story. 'I see you boys are getting killed by your own gas,' she sneered in one of her nightly broadcasts.

The whole thing was covered up for years. Even today, the full details of what actually happened aren't known.

So this is why I guess Norm is always smiling or joking when I see him. 'Every day's a bonus,' he reckons.

He should have been killed four times — on the 'Test Bank', on the raft, while on the dock he should have been blown back into the harbour amongst the mustard gas.

But fourthly, all along the breakwater hundreds, possibly thousands, of 380mm shells were stacked — waiting to go onto the destroyers and battleships.

When the *John L. Motley* went up, the tidal wave washed them all into the sea. If one bomb had landed amongst them it would have almost blown away the entire heel of Italy.

And to quote Norm again: 'I'd still be on my way to Mars.'

Instead, he landed two doors up from me. It's not a bad yarn, and you can get the entire version in Dan Lane's book.

Family SPLITS: no LAUGHING matter

Writing a column where you sometimes try to see the humorous side of things, it's only appropriate certain lines must be drawn.

One thing I don't believe is funny, is the break-up of families. Battered women going through divorces. Husbands sent to the wall. Children torn apart in bitter custody battles. The acrimony of alimony settlements.

There's nothing funny about any of this. It's one of the few things I agree with Fred Nile about, when he says we should do everything we can to preserve the family unit.

And this was the week I wanted to write about John Hewson, a.k.a. Dr Who. Only instead of a Tardis, this doctor blasts around in a Ferrari.

Apart from him being the most colourless speaker Parliament's ever seen, my most vivid recollection of Dr Hewson was on *Fast Forward*, being interviewed by Pixie-Anne Wheatley, when she asked him how the Daleks were treating him.

Hewson didn't have a clue what she was on about. 'My dialect?' he said. 'The way I speak?'

'No. The Daleks,' said Pixie. 'You know. Titter-titter-titter.'

For a man of the people, Hewson doesn't even know what they show on the ABC. Wouldn't know a Dalek if he tripped over one. Wouldn't know K9 if it had an atomic screwdriver jammed in its date. Watching him on *Fast Forward* you'd think he'd just been hatched that morning.

Besides looking like a bit of a wally on the box, the other thing I wanted to write about was 'his belligerent assault on the Australian Council of Social Services', to quote Don Chipp in the *Sunday Telegraph.*

Hewson wants to revamp the social security system, which is okay by me if he wants to get rid of all the morons bludging on it. But I haven't got a clue what he wants to do. No-one has. Not even Yoda — and he teaches Jedi Knights.

Does Hewson want to gas the poor, drown batches of kittens, disband the Salvation Army? Anyone who denies the Salvos a few dollars is a dropkick. Then he wants to introduce a goods and services tax on top of what they rip us off for now. Food, clothes, medicine. Imagine having to pay an extra 15 per cent on a bag of ganja, if you can find one. Plus your piss.

Then his mate Peter Reith accuses us of being a nation of tax-dodging bludgers! Why wouldn't you avoid paying any extra tax when you see their performances in that billion-dollar palace we built them?

How about, instead of ripping us poor bludgers off all the time, they do something about their own waste and extravagance like their government car costs and VIP jets?

I admit, apart from a couple of NSW Independents, politicians of either party are not my cup of tea. And Hewson wants to lead the country. Of course my views on Dr Hewson could be tainted slightly by the awful bollocking he's received in the media over the way he split up with his wife.

I didn't see the *60 Minutes* thing, but I thought fair enough, if she's a nagging battleaxe with a face like a mangey doberman I don't blame him. But I saw snippets on the news and she's quite an attractive, bright woman — even for a brunette.

His three kids didn't actually look like members of some colour gang either. Why leave a family like this? Especially at Xmas.

Evidently it was to further his political aspirations. Political aspirations?

Poor Bob Menzies must roll over in his grave every time Hewson opens his mouth.

Of course, Hewson isn't the only man to leave his wife and family. There are heaps. Take Paul Hogan for instance. He did something similar, only he had five kids and didn't leave at Xmas.

But why again? Oges' wife is a better sort than Hewson's — she's a blonde for a start. Wears good gear, tarts her hair up. I reckon if I took her to the pictures and she had a pair of black stockings on I'd put my hand on her knee.

Yet Hogan left her for a 28-year-old American woman he'd barely met. It's hard to figure out. Of course, it's a credit to both men they never left their wives and families destitute.

Noelene Hogan doesn't actually live in a caravan park at Umina and she'll never starve. It's doubtful she ever did. And

I doubt if the Hewsons get around with a sack picking up aluminium cans out of garbage tins.

But it's no laughing matter. The break-up of the family unit is a sad and terrible thing, whether you're Opposition leader or a famous movie star.

DON'T give 0017s their LICENCE to SWILL

I was watching TV the other night and who should bob up on the screen, in an ad trying to stop kids getting pissed off their faces, but my old mate Angry Anderson.

Actually, Angry isn't an old mate of mine, I've only met him a few times. But, despite the tattoos and slightly menacing appearance, he's one of the most intelligent, articulate people I've been lucky enough to meet.

If Angry shows his concern for kids, or the environment or for anything to do with making a better Australia, he's genuine and means it right from his heart.

As far as dissuading kids from getting pissed off their faces or trying to stop under-age drinking, he might as well go and bang his little bald head against the nearest wall.

It's like trying to stop the imbeciles from smoking or picking up their rubbish after them.

Kids these days know all there is to know, plus they've got their rights.

But as a disinterested observer, standing back, watching the youth of Australia pickle their brains, I'll give you some examples of under-age drinking and getting blind out of your mind. And I should know. I had my first beer in a pub when I was 15.

It was the Imperial Hotel in Paddington. I was a pimply-faced apprentice butcher and we'd just finished training one night at the local Police Boys' Club. The beer tasted like a glass of cloudy ammonia after a tomcat had pissed in it, but that didn't matter.

As far as I was concerned, I was one of the boys, I was at the bar having a beer with the men.

I used to sneak the odd beer now and again at the Royal Hotel in Bondi, but this big, horrible detective who knew me and liked me kept booting my arse out of the place in front of all the other drinkers.

I didn't realise it at the time, as I'd limp down Denham Street holding my arse, but he was doing me a favour. But the biggest favour done to me in regards to under-age drinking, was when I was 17. Still a pimply-faced apprentice butcher.

It was a Friday and one of the local butchers was going interstate, so a few blokes went down to the Bondi Hotel to give him a send off — and I was invited.

I had it made. I could breast the bar with all the local butchers. The men. I was only sorry I couldn't wear my coat and apron and bring a couple of steak knives.

So here I am with all these huge blokes who needed a gallon of beer each to soak up the four T-bones and six lamb chops they'd eaten that day.

Next thing I was in a shout and, in less than an hour, I'd drunk eight schooners.

I wished them all the best then left, saying I'd catch up with them tomorrow.

I spewed on every corner and outside every block of flats between the Bondi Hotel and Lamrock Avenue. By the time I'd made it to my front door, my face was the colour of bad shit and the only thing coming out of me was something that looked like brake fluid.

I was in bed by 7 p.m. and my boss was banging on the door at 6.30 a.m. the next morning to get me to come to work.

Since then I've never been an after-work drinker. I like nothing better than a social drink or to get a bit roaring at parties. But down the pub for a couple of hundred schooners with the boys after work? Thanks a lot, but no thanks.

Another example of under-age drinking. A bloke I know had a step-daughter — we'll call her Terri. Terri looked like a taller version of Michelle Pfeiffer, only with longer legs and bigger tits. She went to Terrigal High School and, according to her younger sister, she was 17.

I never used to perv on Terri. But if ever she was in the backyard hanging out the washing, I'd always give the sundeck a sweep and keep an eye on her just in case she fell over or a snake bit her or something. I even gave her a lift home from school a couple of times.

Well, what's a man supposed to do when he sees the girl next door walking home in the heat wearing one of those heavy school uniforms?

Isn't that what Neighbourhood Watch is all about?

I was working part-time then as a DJ in a club in Gosford. It was another Friday night and who should come marching in, looking stunning, but Terri.

The first person she saw was me, so she walked over and the first thing I said was: 'Hey, Terri. You're not 18.'

Just like a young kid confronted by the truth, she said: 'Yeah, I'm 15. But don't say you saw me, willya?' My jaw nearly fell into the Duran Duran–Go-Go's mix I had coming up.

Here was the girl next door, in a disco, having a drink and she's 15. What could I do? Be Mr Nark, the old shit next door, and have her thrown out? I just did my job, throwing on Eurythmics and INXS.

By about midnight though, young Terri was starting to look like a second-hand dressing table. Her colour was starting to fade, her legs were wobbly and her drawers were getting a bit loose.

What happened to her on the night I don't know, the last I saw she was standing at the bar, pissed, with all these blokes looking at her like they were Zeke Wolf and she was a tray of lamb cutlets.

I didn't see her back at the disco as I left soon after, but I bumped into her down at the old Florida Hotel a few times and I remember her saying to me one night, in good, drunken Strine: 'Hey, Bob. Thesebourn'cokesarrorightarnay?'

Another example: four kids, aged 15 to 18, just rolled a stolen car in Sydney's suburban Lakemba. All four killed. Incinerated. They'd just drunk 24 cans of beer and a cask of wine.

I know it sounds callous, but I don't feel sorry for them. I feel sorry for the poor mug whose car they stole and I'd feel a lot sorrier if they'd rolled the car through a schoolteacher or a nun taking a class of schoolkids on an outing, killing about 10.

So, if I'm so smart, what's the answer to under-age drinking and kids getting pissed off their heads through peer pressure? Even if it's only for the sake of the poor bastards working behind the bar or in bottle shops, who get pinched just for doing their job when some kid walks in with someone else's ID?

Well one idea would be to copy the Yanks and raise the age limit for drinking to 21.

'Aargh! Boo! Hiss!' Already I can hear the screams from any 18-year-olds reading this column. 'You miserable shit! Drop dead you old spackattack.'

But don't worry, zitheads. The breweries know how much money you bludge off your oldies and there's as much chance of the age limit being raised as Roger Rogerson getting the cleaning contract at Goulburn Police Academy. But it's not a bad idea.

When I was in America I remember going into these bars and discos. There might have been a couple of 19-year-olds who snuck in, but there were definitely no 15- and 17-year-olds pissed out of their brains, arguing and chundering all over the place. Everybody seemed to be having a good time.

People were actually having intelligent conversations. Others who have visited the States have also remarked on this weird phenomenon to me.

But there is a compromise — sort of. Why not let some premises, if they want to, have a special licence so that you have to be aged 21 to be on those premises? Call it an American licence for want of a better word.

There'd still be heaps of places the zitheads could go and get pissed out of their brains, still sneak in on someone else's ID and pass for 18.

But there would also be these other places — bars, bottleshops etc., where you would have to be 21 to get served.

A few 19-year-olds still would probably try to sneak in. But it would keep the 15- and 17-year-olds out. They might pass for 18, but try as they might, no 15- or 17-year-old can look and act 21.

Definitely not pigshead the pimply-faced apprentice butcher or Terri the girl next door.

Cotton-picking GENIUS

You know, sometimes I have to sit back and ask myself why I'm so clever. Why I'm such a genius. A modest one, but a genius all the same. One astute reader even suggested I run for Parliament.

Is it the way I look at things that makes me such a genius: a sort of spaced-out, lateral thinking?

I look at things from a working person's point of view, not the view of some politician or bureaucrat in an ivory tower in Canberra.

This column will prove once and for all why I'm a genius as, in one fell swoop, I sort out two of the biggest problems facing Australia today, and possibly the world: the environment and racism.

First, the environment. Apart from pollution and land degradation the most vexing problem would be the destruction of our rainforests.

I'm in no way against logging — I'm for the timber industry and keeping the small sawmills going.

But I'm totally against woodchipping, especially to make more money for those stinking Japanese. Turning rainforests into wrapping paper and chopsticks is an abomination. Fifty per cent of our rainforests are gone forever.

Now one in every three of what trees we've got left goes to those lovely, dolphin-slaughtering Japs to wrap presents in or sell back to us at some exorbitant profit to them.

But, according to the information I have, the whole deal with the forest industry is to get in and rape the guts out of what's left because in less than five years it won't be worth the effort.

Bolivia, Chile and Brazil had the foresight to grow millions of hectares of eucalypt trees and they'll have that much plantation timber the price will plummet and what's left of ours will be worth nothing.

So any timber workers out there who think the timber industry or the National Party have got your welfare at heart, you can't see any further than the top of your schooner glass. In five years you'll be redundant. But we'll still have a timber industry of our own because we're not going to miss a few trees here and there — and that's a good thing.

Meanwhile we have to recycle what paper we use, but the answer to the whole problem has been in our hands all the time. Banknotes. Did you know banknotes aren't made out of paper, they're made out of cotton? Now what have we got in the middle of Australia? Millions of acres of scrub, with the potential for thousands of artesian bores underneath.

Why not flood the middle of Australia with bore water, grow millions of hectares of cotton and make millions of tonnes of the toughest paper available?

Use solar power and windmills to make it as self-sufficient and environmentally friendly as possible. Run in a rail system and, in a few years, all we'd be sending out of the middle of Australia would be billions of dollars worth of paper straight onto the export market.

We'd still have our rainforests, and all the woodchippers could find work in the parks and wildlife department making just as much money as they are now — showing tourists around while they rob them blind selling souvenirs.

Now, what else have we got in Australia that's a tough fibre and definitely a @#$% curse from hell? Lantana. I hate it.

I used to clear it for a living and it fights back. You can rip it out but you end up in full nelsons and Indian deathlocks trying to hack it up. It fights better than a battalion of Ghurkhas. I reckon throughout Australia there'd be 100 million tonnes of lantana. Why not start up a lantana eradication scheme and pulp it too?

A schoolkid told me there's more fibre in half a tonne of lantana than in four tonnes of woodchips and I believe him.

The stinkin' shit grows anywhere too. Why not take some out to the middle of Australia, grow it around the cotton fields for protection and pulp the whole lot up together?

We can't afford to do it? We spend millions to try a few old war criminals, we give more millions away in overseas aid to people that hate us and we blew a billion dollars on a new Parliament House.

If we can't get this thing going, with overseas investment, we all need rooting. It's a good idea well worth a try and it's simplicity itself.

Now, onto the other problem, racism. Who are the biggest whingers — always wanting to put the boot into poor old whitey?

The Chinese students aren't bad. But the government just gave them an $82 million refund on some university fees and let

10,000 into Australia, putting them straight on social security, so they're happy.

The Kooris aren't bad whingers. But after 200 years of rape and murder and the possibility of the canteen on Arukun being closed, the Abos are entitled to have a beef.

But the biggest whingers have to be the American Negroes or Afro-Americans as they now like to be called. Though you don't know what to call them — blacks, negroes, niggers with attitude — there's no pleasing them. But they've got the right to whinge, the poor bludgers.

Seventy per cent of the gaol population in America is black. They flunk school, they're badly educated, they can't get work. They either live in swamps in the south or ghettos in the north. They're heavily into crack-cocaine and run around shooting each other. A black kid's lucky to reach 21.

Even other minority groups are against them. When a black stabbed an Australian Jew to death in Brooklyn the blacks called out to the Jews, 'Hitler should have finished the job'. The Jews yelled back, 'Jews invented the wheelbarrow so niggers could learn to walk on their hind legs'.

Disgraceful racist comments and I'm glad I wasn't there to witness them. I truly feel sorry for the blacks in America. I feel they're crying out for something, missing something. And you know what the answer to the black racial problem is? Bring back slavery.

Now, before you all go off the deep end and call me another Hitler, think this over logically, to quote Mr Spock.

Look at those blacks running around with machine-guns, into crack, prostitution, killing other brothers. They're stuffed.

But look at all those old Shirley Temple and Clara Bow movies. Look at *Gone With The Wind* and old episodes of the *Jack Benny Show*.

The blacks in them were as happy as Larry, out in the fields working in the sun and fresh air, eating watermelons and playing their banjos. Shuffling around saying, 'Yes massa, no massa'. Everyone singing 'Ol' Man River' and 'Swing Low Sweet Chariot'. Happy as pigs in shit — they had it made.

Of course, you couldn't go back to the original conditions. No whipping, no chains, no burning crosses. This is ACTU slavery. A 40-hour week and weekends free.

They could retain their Afro names, dress and walk like they want. Have ghetto blasters. Any Rastas could grow a bit of ganja.

I don't know how much a slave would cost these days, but after checking prices back in 1700 and allowing for inflation and the cost-price index, I reckon a good big buck with decent teeth would be worth around $500.

The Australian government could buy 200,000. And what are slaves good for? Working in cotton fields. And where are all the cotton fields? Right in the middle of Australia, like I said. Millions of hectares of them.

We ship all those slaves out here, save them from life in the ghettos being eaten by rats, and put them to work in the sun picking cotton for 'massa'.

And if they don't like it — stiff shit! There's all that lantana growing around the place so they can't get out. It's perfect.

There's another spin-off too. Think of all the sensational new blues and Motown music we'd get. The music industry would make more millions, CD prices would come down and everybody would be happy.

Especially the blacks … plenty to eat, out in the sun and dancing around on the weekends like toady-frogs. It's perfect. Instead of niggaz with attitude, they'd be niggaz with plentitude.

So there you have it. Two problems fixed for the price of one. And you wonder why that bloke wanted me in Parliament.

THE LAW is a DOPE

Mark Geyer is a big, bad rugby league forward. He's as big as a house, fit, strong and wild, the complete football cyborg pumped out by the sports machine the crowd loves. A real meat-head league player.

Personally, I like the big cheeseburger. He's played for his State, his country and helped win a grand final. He plays the game hard and fast with plenty of controlled aggression, which the punters love.

Best of all he sticks it up those rotten Queensland cane toads — especially King Wally. One State of Origin game he had Wally that furious I thought he was going to take to big Mark with his handbag.

I wish Geyer played for Easts. But the best thing with him is what you see is what you get.

Like me, he's no rocket scientist, but he does his best.

When he made that speech and thanked all the Penrith fans for their support, saying they couldn't have won the grand final without them, he wasn't just playing to the crowd. He meant every word. You could see the emotion welling up inside him.

Same when he talks to the kids. He gets a bit tongue-tied but he does his best. He is what he is and I don't think that's a bad sign in a bloke.

At the moment though, Geyer is involved in the most unbelievable hoo-ha imaginable.

According to the papers, Geyer is alleged to have tested positive to marijuana — even though it's not 100 per cent certain if he did.

Big bloody deal.

But he's been suspended, fined and pilloried in the press by certain pisshead journalists and even had to get Chris Murphy as his lawyer. They've done everything but draw and quarter him and stick his head on a pike.

You'd think he'd robbed a bank and then got caught with his hand up Orphan Annie's dress. All these pious old bores in the league hierarchy are jumping up and down. The image of the game must be upheld, they thunder.

Image? Rugby league is sponsored by booze and cigarettes, the two biggest killer drugs in the country.

And a couple of old players told me that if you opened up a few closets around the league hierarchy a lot of skeletons would come rattling out holding SP bookmaking sheets.

Geyer sure doesn't look like a mullhead to me. A meat-head, maybe. But what if he did prove positive to pot? It's not as if he filled himself full of speed, coke or steroids before a game.

It's stupid. Even Mal Meninga, an ex-cop, and Wayne Bennett, the Queensland coach, said it's not worth all the trouble the league is going to.

The thing is, Geyer doesn't need Chris Murphy to get him off this bum rap. All he's got to do is say he was at a party and there was a bunch of mullheads there getting into a few joints and he's a victim of passive smoking.

It's a fact. I don't smoke. I hate cigarettes. But after a night in a bar or disco, I'd have enough nicotine in me to say I'd had 20 puffers — due to passive smoking.

It's been proved. And they say the THC from pot stays in your body fats for months. If Murphy can't beat this one he should give the game away.

But the whole drama around pot, the killer drug that's going to destroy us all, is ridiculous. I've already written a column on it and I've had people write to me about it. I even suggested they let the Kooris grow it and keep the profits. Anything.

And it's not as if I haven't had experience with the 'erb. In the '70s, when we used to get it through those kindly Italians in Griffith for $30 an ounce, we'd smoke enough dacca on the weekend to stuff a mattress. But we still went to work on Monday and I'm still here.

Like my mates, I've been busted. Had the cops charging in with a warrant, guns at the ready. Up goes your mattress, all your clothes get reefed out of your wardrobe, they go through all your personal things. It's great.

Then you waste the time of another six cops, a prosecutor, your lawyer, a magistrate — all that paperwork for a $250 fine. It that's not a waste of time, what is? And I still can't figure out why it is.

If you're a rotten, thieving heroin addict you can go to a needle exchange and get a free prick, a cup of coffee and no questions asked. Why can't mullheads go to a bong exchange when their bong clogs up and get another one? Isn't this discriminatory?

I'm certain there's a conspiracy around pot. Take what's been happening in Coffs Harbour. A huge number of ordinary, rate-paying citizens have been trying to stop a stinking sewerage outfall going into the ocean where they live.

They weren't so-called hippies, but old ladies, blokes and women with kids, worrying about their future. And the cops just bashed and brutalised them. Real heroes.

Some were even strip-searched by cops hoping they'd find a bit of pot. If they found any, the cops and council aldermen who want the outfall could say they're all druggies. That's how it works.

Same with the citizens trying to save what trees we've got left. They're out there in front of the bulldozers and, next thing, up lumbers some 12-beers-a-day moron, with a stomach as large as his brain is small, holding a sign saying: 'We Want Jobs — Not Drugs'. And more than likely it's written in crayon.

So the law, oppressive as it is, definitely suits the cops and the politicians at the moment. But there are others who couldn't really give a stuff about dope and would rather be out after the heroin and coke dealers. I know I'd rather be.

So, if I was a politician, what would I do to make a serious dent in the true drug problem? Putting heroin, coke and speed into the too-hard basket for the time being, let's start with pot.

The first thing I'd do is burn every copy of that poster of Allen Ginsberg, the US poet, holding a sign saying 'Pot Is Fun'. At $400 an ounce, pot definitely ain't fun.

Then I'd take the scientific and moral high-ground. I'd start by saying that seeing the Jamaican Government is making medicine out of marijuana — because it reduces ocular pressure and can ultimately cure glaucoma and asthma, and ease the pain for cancer sufferers — cabinet will be forced to have another think.

Seeing as pot's easy on your eyes it's going to be classed as a soft drug.

But if there are dills out there who still want to smoke the shit, it's going to cost you. We're sick of tying up men and resources.

So, if you're working and over 21, you pay $100 for a licence and you can grow enough in your backyard to keep you going.

If anybody asks, just say it's for your eyes or for your grandma's asthma. And that's it. Piss off.

Veg out, listen to your silly bloody music and just leave the rest of us alone. At least you're working and not breaking into houses.

If not completely decriminalising it, I'd take the stigma out of pot. Even if it's only for people like footballers and Paul McCartney. Look at poor Paul. He got busted in Japan with half an elbow and now everybody hates him and nobody buys his records any more. See what I mean?

The 500,000 mullheads who buy a licence will provide $50 million in government money every year. I'd run the thing through the police revenue service where you pay your traffic fines.

Then I'd have an extradition treaty drawn up with Iran and send any heroin or coke dealers that get caught over there to be tried by an Islamic court. Being a politician, you have to foster ethnic and religious goodwill. And that's about it.

Even the ex-Premier of NSW, Neville Wran, was quoted in the paper as saying, 'Some form of legalising might be sensible. Certainly marijuana.' But would something like this ever happen? There's a good chance.

Firstly, they've legalised brothels in NSW. This means you can go into a whorehouse dressed as Batman, pork some moll wearing a school uniform while she whips you with a dead octopus and it's all sweet.

Could this be any worse than sitting back stoned in your own home listening to old Moody Blues CDs? Along with the devos, the cops might get sick of chasing the mullheads, too.

Secondly, if you're talking about politicians, you have to think like a politician. And remember, to a politician a person is not a human being. You're a vote with skin wrapped around it.

One day, some politician is going to think that with the $50 million coming in every year and the money the government's saving by not running around chasing mullheads, there are 500,000 votes out there. And you won't lose any other votes because nobody gives a shit about mullheads anyway.

Some politician's only got to say he's dropping the tax on Tally Hos — let alone decriminalise the shit — and half a million votes fall into the bag.

And thirdly, I have actually drunk with members of the NSW and Commonwealth police. A lot of them read my books.

I was having a drink with some the other day and overheard one cop remark that, in line with all this drug testing, there's talk of introducing it into the police force. And it's not going down all that well.

At first I couldn't understand this — until I thought on it. With all that white powder floating around as evidence it would be a bit hard to explain if you registered positive to the okey or hammer.

But does this also mean the career of some proudly serving member of the police force is over if they test positive to the old dacca, even though it's possible they're passive smoking victims?

What a terrible thought. That's another reason they might have to take the stigma out of it.

TALL TALES and FAREWELLS

Regular readers of this column might be wondering what's going on. I kick off in the black-and-white section then I go to full glossy colour, next thing I'm back in the black and white.

The column is certainly colourful enough without adding any extras. Actually, it was my idea. I felt lonely in the colour section and wanted to get back next to my old mate, Paul B. Kidd. I get back and Kidd couldn't jump into my colour spot quick enough. He's good.

So, instead of Australia's fishiest bloke, I'm stuck next to Jacko. Not Jacko the good-humoured Pom in *Brush Strokes*, but Mark Jackson, the mouth from the south. It's enough to make you want to throw in the towel.

What can you say about Jacko's column? He doesn't take any prisoners. Troy Waters can't fight, Greg Williams and Gerard Healy are traitors and should be put in front of a firing squad, Healy wearing his favourite dress. The Balinese are horrible little toads and he's suing Kevin Bloody Wilson for saying those

Energizer TV commercials reminded him of Billy Idol with prostate gland trouble.

I'll say one thing for Jacko. He's done something I haven't. Played first-grade football for a leading Melbourne club. Even if it is only kick-basketball. Actually, the phenomenon of Aussie Rules and the way those Victorians revere the kick-basketballers has always had me stuffed. They treat them like gods.

I don't wish to speak ill of the dead, but when that bloke went under a car and killed himself he had a blood alcohol reading that would have launched the Challenger. Yet you'd have thought they were burying Gandhi. Thousands jammed the street carting a coffin around with some Collingwood polka blaring in the background.

When a poker machine mysteriously landed on George Piper's head during a brawl in the Balmain Kodocs Club and they had to bury him, there was a fair sort of a crowd. But nothing like that thing in Melbourne.

But good luck to Jacko. There was even talk at one time of Jacko playing the lead if they ever made a movie out of my books. But after watching the *Highwayman*, I feel it would be demeaning to the man.

Jacko is destined for better things than playing some yobbo Queensland hillbilly in an Australian, meat-pie western.

But I've got a book coming out this month — *Davo's Little Something*. It's not a Les Norton. It's about a butcher-turned-serial killer who murders 30 skinheads. If they make a movie out of it, there might be a part for Jacko. As a hindquarter of beef. A meat-role.

But talking about throwing in the towel — that's what's happening. This is my last column for *People*. I'm racking my cue, rolling my swag, pulling in my line. Grasshopper can finally snatch the literary pebble from Master's hand and is leaving the temple. It is time to go. It had to happen sooner or later. I was initially only supposed to be here six months, and it's over two years.

I'm off now to concentrate on the next book.

Before I go. May I just say, if there's a young lady out there, a non-smoker, who would like to help me with a bit of research and learn how to write a book in the meantime, give me a whistle care of Terrigal Post Office. You know how to whistle don't you?

So how do you say goodbye? The funny thing about this column, it wasn't so much just my opinion — I was a conduit for the average punter. I'd be somewhere and someone would say something about someone, or something they saw on TV or read in the papers, and I'd more or less echo their sentiments.

And didn't we echo some? Trish Goddard, Robbo, Alan Jones, Hinch, The TRG, 2JJJ, public servants, Kooris, the gay and ethnic lobbies, Pickering, Skase, Bond, politicians …

I can't see myself ever getting another gig on the ABC and there's no way I'll get my hair cut in Oxford Street. I don't think I would have run out of subjects. Not while I kept bumping into punters from all walks of life wanting to give me GBH of the earhole. But I remember saying I was going to write about my great-great-grandfather Richard Bigmore Barrett, the remittance man who tamed the Central Coast in the 1800s. What a bloke. So I think it's only appropriate that my last column should be dedicated to him and the story of how he lost his first fortune.

Bigmore had money when he arrived from England, but he made most of it gathering cedar at Ourimbah and running punts on the Hawkesbury River. He had six kids to two wives but the apple of his eye was his manservant and faithful companion,

Tjalkaleiri, an Aboriginal from the Wurrunnunah tribe. 'Chalky' as Bigmore called him.

Chalky was drinking methylated spirits and playing a gumleaf in Mann Street, Gosford when Bigmore took him under his wing. He cleaned him up, looked after him and they became inseparable. Bigmore treated Chalky like a son and to Chalky, Bigmore was the father the earlier white settlers gave a bag of poisoned flour to in Woy Woy. They went everywhere and did everything together, and Bigmore owed much of his good fortune to Tjalkaleiri's prowess as an expert bushman and tracker. The only thing Bigmore didn't know about Chalky was that all his tribe were coprophiliacs.

One summer they were five days' horse ride north of Newcastle, going through the sandhills towards Taree, looking for a gold reef supposed to be in the area. They passed Broughton Island and were camped one night when they were attacked by a pack of wild dingoes. Bigmore and Chalky fought them off but the horses bolted, leaving them with one water-bottle, six dry biscuits and a 10-day walk back to Newcastle. If they made it.

They set off the next morning and, before they left, Bigmore handed Chalky three biscuits. Chalky told him to keep them, just give him a bit of water now and again. He'd be all right.

Bigmore couldn't believe it. His faithful manservant Tjalkaleiri would starve to death so his master could live. Tearful stuff.

They'd been walking for three days when they stopped for the night. Bigmore went for a crap. He came back to the campfire, sat there for a while and couldn't find his watch. Thinking he might have dropped it when he had a dump, he walked back to find the turd was gone. Bigmore thought this a bit odd.

Back at the campfire, Chalky was sitting crosslegged, picking his teeth with a twig, so Bigmore asked him: 'Hey Chalky. Did you see what happened to my turd?'

And Chalky replied, 'I ate it boss.'

'You ate it?'

'Yeah. I eat shit. All the Wurrus do, if we're hungry and there's nothing around.'

Bigmore sat down dumbfounded. Then he said, 'Chalky, if we get out of this, we're going to make a fortune.' Chalky continued picking his teeth, shrugged, and thought no more about it.

The next morning, they were walking along the beach and as fate would have it, Blaxland, Wentworth and Lawson flew overhead in a hot-air balloon, with a couple of developers, catching the nor'-easter from Taree to Newcastle. They saw Bigmore and Chalky waving on the beach, picked them up and flew them to Newcastle. The boys were saved.

Bigmore couldn't get back to the Central Coast quick enough and get the ball rolling.

He got 1000 pounds out of the bank and made his first strike at the Union Hotel in Gosford, setting up bets that he had this Koori who could eat faecal matter.

Of course, the locals didn't believe him. No-one would eat shit. Not even an Abo. They packed the Union. Bigmore handed a plate to the crowd for anyone to drop a turd on. They got one and Chalky tore into it.

Richard Bigmore was on a roll. They did pubs on the Central Coast. Workers clubs in Newcastle and Cessnock. Chalky didn't even have to finish the whole thing if he didn't want to. The smell alone from some of them was enough to make everyone want to settle and get out of the place.

Then Bigmore got them both tuxedos and they started doing gentlemen's clubs in Sydney. They knocked over City

Tattersalls and Bigmore had 150,000 pounds. When who should arrive in Sydney but William Randolph Hearst, the American publishing tycoon. He heard what was going on and proposed a bet — 150,000 pounds. Bigmore accepted.

This was now the talk of Sydney and a crowd of thousands was expected, so it was going to be an outdoor event. They'd only done hotels and clubs so far, but Bigmore couldn't see any difference so he and Hearst settled for Sydney's Domain, near Mrs Macquarie's Chair.

It was midday Sunday, one of those sticky overcast summer days in Sydney; thousands of people crowded round a small table with a plate; Bigmore and Chalky in their tuxedos.

It was Hearst's day, so he elected to have a dump. Fair enough. It wasn't that big a turd. The boys had seen plenty bigger. Bigmore gave Chalky a wink and a thumbs up. 'Go for it mate. This is the big one.' Chalky whipped his monogrammed spoon out of his tux and was about to get into it when he froze and his face suddenly went green. He dropped the spoon, leapt up from the table and ran through the crowd with his hands over his mouth.

Well that was it. Bigmore had done his arse. Plus. The Yank roared laughing, scooped up the money and gave Bigmore the finger.

There was pandemonium but Bigmore was screaming. He charged through the crowd after Chalky and found him down at the seawall, heaving his guts up into Sydney Harbour.

Bigmore could hardly get the words out. 'Chalky, what happened? We've pulled this stroke all over NSW. The big one comes up and you blow it.'

But, despite his anger, Bigmore couldn't help but feel remorse for his faithful companion. 'Chalky, mate. What went wrong?'

Chalky wiped his mouth and looked up at his master. 'I'm sorry boss. I couldn't. It was covered in flies.'

Then for the first time in their lives, Bigmore swore at and struck his best friend. He punched Chalky right in the face, bashed his head into the wall and kicked him in the ribs. 'Well why didn't you #@*%! tell me, and I would have got you another one. You dopey black #@*%!'

There have been variations of this tale over the years, but that's the truth and don't believe anything else you might hear.

And that's where I have to leave you.

Looking back, I reckon this column had its moments. So what do …?

Dates published in *People* magazine:

So why doesn't Jack the lad get a real job? *November 7, 1989*
I might be a racist, but… *November 21, 1989*
Poofs on parade *November 28, 1989*
Tall poppies deserve short shrift *December 5, 1989*
Barrett's gone a-punting *December 12, 1989*
The Wellington's on the other foot *December 19, 1989*
The politics of pot *January 16, 1990*
Public dis-service *January 23, 1990*
Take Derryn Hinch… please *February 13, 1990*
It's time to munch our moggies *February 20, 1990*
A plague on puffers *February 27, 1990*
TV ads… the real thing??? *March 6, 1990*
Bore it up 'em, Bruce *March 13, 1990*
Duck! It's the silly season again *March 20, 1990*
Me nude! You must be stark raving mad *April 24, 1990*
Real men save whales *May 1, 1990*
Who's jack of Robbo? *May 8, 1990*
Keystone Kops meet Police Academy 6 *May 16, 1990*
Of big wets and bigger hearts *May 30, 1990*
Love thy neighbour *June 13, 1990*
Living with Derryn the dunnart *June 20, 1990*
A week's a long time in Uki *June 27, 1990*
The banks: bloody-minded blood suckers *July 4, 1990*
The perfect murder *July 25, 1990*
Kill two birds with one stone *August 8, 1990*
Cross my heart and hope to diet *August 15, 1990*
Casey's wace isn't won *August 29, 1990*
Jaws 5: The butcher takes off *September 19, 1990*
Snowed under *October 17, 1990*
Better a white racist bastard than a black *October 24, 1990*
A McCullough to cut the deadwood *November 7, 1990*
Mike, I'm not a racist… just bored *November 21, 1990*
Hang on… I was only joking *November 28, 1990*
Sleaze stays when the party's over *December 5, 1990*
The last hurrah for Bondi Brad *December 12, 1990*
Aunty's aces by me *January 16, 1991*
Madonna: plenty to grumble about *January 23, 1991*
How to be an awther *February 13, 1991*
This isn't union bashing but… *March 6, 1991*
What are you laughin' at? *March 20, 1991*
Ayatollah of the airwaves *April 3, 1991*
Starstruck? Not us Scorpios *April 17, 1991*
Mad Wax before Thunderdome *April 24, 1991*
Say your prayers varmints! *May 1, 1991*
Ambos have to cop it sweet *May 15, 1991*
Racist yes, sexist fine, tobacconist no! *June 12, 1991*
A tour de Bondi *July 17, 1991*
Kakadu, the new Eden *August 7, 1991*
The republic starts to flag *August 14, 1991*
Leave no turn unstoned *September 4, 1991*
An artful dodger *September 11, 1991*
I'm pulling for ya, Pee Wee *October 9, 1991*
I saw that and I'm telling *October 16, 1991*
Dr Doug meets his match *October 23, 1991*
Digger drops a bombshell *October 30, 1991*
Family splits: no laughing matter *November 13, 1991*
Don't give 0017s their licence to swill *November 27, 1991*
Cotton-picking genius *December 11, 1991*
The law is a dope *January 1, 1992*
Tall tales and farewells *January 8, 1992*